JUST HIT IT

Just Hit It

OUR EQUIPMENT AND OUR GAME

Frank Thomas

with Jeff Neuman

FRANKLY

FRANKLY PUBLICATIONS
CHAMPIONSGATE, FLORIDA

To Haggis

And to those who have truly supported us and our cause
– Frankly, I thank you.

FRANKLY

A FRANKLY PUBLICATION

ISBN: 978-0-615-18109-7

Frankly Publications are available for group discounts and premium editions. For more information, contact Frankly Publications, 8390 ChampionsGate Boulevard, #100, ChampionsGate, FL 33896, or via email at www.franklygolf.com.

Designed by Pam Pollack

Printed in the United States of America.
First edition.

CONTENTS

Foreword by Jack Nicklaus *1*

Prologue *3*

1. Meta-*Fore!* *13*

2. Implements *33*

3. Three Innovations that Changed the Game *47*

4. Time Out for Science *71*

5. Equipment Essentials *91*

6. By the Rules *131*

7. Saving the Game *157*

Foreword

Any time you are looking for a lively, well-informed conversation (or even good-spirited debate) about the game of golf, you might want to seek out Frank Thomas. Frank has been involved in so many aspects of golf — as an equipment innovator, a rules-maker and administrator, and as a passionate writer and commentator — that you're likely to come away with some new knowledge and perspective on your long-held assumptions.

I first met Frank in the mid-1970s, when he was beginning his work as the Technical Director of the USGA. I was sitting in the locker room at Southern Hills during the U.S. Open, and he came up to me and asked me if he could have some of my golf balls. He was doing a broad spectrum of tests in those days to make sure that the balls we were competing with had the same specifications as the ones submitted to the USGA for approval. The balls I handed him passed their test, of course, but I'll let him tell you about the other results he found — details he didn't share with me for over twenty years.

It is ironic that our first conversation was about golf balls, because we've been arguing about the ball for years now. Simply put, I think today's ball goes too far, and that it's changed the way the game is played. If you look at who dominates the professional game today, it's the "bombers." A premium once placed on accuracy has now been placed on distance. It doesn't make a difference where today's players hit the ball, because they are getting so close to the greens, and left with such short approaches, that they can make birdie out of any rough. Thousands of golf courses and great championship venues have been rendered obsolete. I firmly believe that if something isn't done about the ball, we're going to have to make every golf course 8,000 or so yards in order to challenge the top players, and that's going to cost millions of dollars in extra land and maintenance for the people who build, own, and manage the courses for tournaments. It's absurd to spend that kind of money, when it would cost so little to rein in the ball, relatively speaking.

Frank disagrees. Frank disagrees with a lot of what's become conventional wisdom about the game. That's fine. He and I have had some very direct conversations about these things, and while I know what I see, Frank approaches things differently — from the perspective of the lab and the test range. He says the Overall Distance Standard, with just a little tweaking, will do enough to control the explosion of distance in the game. I don't know about that; I don't think it is working. When I mentioned to him in a conversation a few years ago that I was sure that today's players were overpowering the golf course in ways we could never do during the majority of my career, he pointed out that I won a long-drive contest in 1963 by hitting the ball 341 yards, with a wound ball and a persimmon driver. (Actually, in this case, he's wrong: I hit it 341 yards and 17 inches.) As always, our conversation was amicable and thought-provoking.

This book is the product of Frank's many years of studying, testing, and, perhaps most important, simply thinking. Reading his book is just like engaging him in a discussion, with the words, ideas, and passion flowing freely. There are few people I know more knowledgeable about the technical aspects of the game of golf, and very few more passionate about the need for integrity and vision in all aspects of the game. Like me, Frank loves the game. He loves the experience of it, and wants to keep it healthy and strong so that it can be enjoyed by everyone for many future generations. In that respect, there is a lot more that Frank and I agree about than disagree. — *Jack Nicklaus*

Prologue

What would you pay for a golf club that is guaranteed to hit every drive 260 yards down the center of the fairway?

I don't mean a club that's simply more forgiving, that will reduce your hook or your slice or give you more distance on your off-center hits. I mean a beautiful boomer into the middle of the short grass, every single time.

There are already plenty of clubs on the market that make promises like this, and they generally cost $400–500 new. You've probably got one in your bag right now. So how much more would you pay to know for certain that you're going to get the results you want? An additional $500? $1,000? More?

I wouldn't pay a penny for such a club.

Are you surprised? Let's think about it for a bit. Yes, the first time you swing this Biggest Big R7-983 Bigfoot, you'll thrill to the sight of the ball soaring into the sky and settling to rest in Position A. Your friends will ooh and aah, you'll walk a little taller, and you might even play the game of your life — though you'll still be on your own for the approach shots, the short game, and the par-threes. For the first time in ages, you're not buying the drinks after the round. The ride home feels shorter somehow. Your wife looks prettier. The kids are better behaved. You are The Man.

But what happens next week? You show up, full of your newfound confidence, swing smartly, sending your opening drive straight and true — and then your brother-in-law steps up with *his* brand new Biggest Big Et Cetera and next thing you know his ball is sharing prime real estate with yours. On every fairway you walk out to the center stripe and have to check the markings to see which ball is his and which is yours. Your step loses some of its spring, your pride and joy feels a little tarnished, your car backfires on the way home, and you're not looking forward quite as much to next week's round. And, sure enough, when the four of you next gather for your usual game, the rest of your foursome drags out *their* Biggest Bigs, and you begin to notice a nasty cluster of divots right down those formerly green paths. Pretty soon, you all agree that there's really no point in bothering to swing this Biggest Big driving club, and so you walk directly from the previous green to a spot 260 yards from the hole's former teeing ground and each drop a ball somewhere away from an existing divot. Your round is quicker since you've chopped off nearly half the course, and your scores are reduced significantly, but you know that something's not right. You consider sleeping in or cleaning the garage next week. Or taking up tennis.

You realize that the great score you recorded when you first used the club was something you bought, not something you earned. There might as well be a rule that lets you pay an extra $20 at the end of your round to take off five shots from your score. The pride you were feeling seems pretty hollow about now.

What's happened is that the game you once enjoyed is no longer your own. The shots you hit aren't yours; they belong to the club. You've taken the value of the effort that led to your best results and exchanged it for the false economy of someone else's certainty. The only thing such a magic club can do is to take all the magic out of the game itself.

Golf club manufacturers seduce us with the promise of implements that will undo our errors, correct our flaws, forgive our sins, and lead us down the straight and narrow. They can't, of course, and that's a good thing — even though we would like to believe they can. Such fantasies have always been part of this complex game's charm And yet, the moment when we realize we would reject an all-correcting club is when we move closest to a true understanding of why we play at all.

We're funny creatures, we humans. We construct our lives so as to eliminate as many obstacles as we possibly can; we smooth our paths, build labor-saving devices, wire our homes so that we can bring the bounty of the world to us with just the click of a mouse. And then we take a whole set of artificial difficulties and obstacles, put them directly in our way so we have to maneuver around and over and through them, and we call it a game.

Why do we play golf? What are we hoping to prove when we do? Is it just a pleasant walk or ride in the country, or is there something more that draws us back to the course time after time?

I believe that we have a subconscious urge to evaluate ourselves. We are constantly driven to test ourselves against some kind of challenge. For some people, nothing short of a trek up the highest mountain will serve to prove our worth to ourselves. For others, struck down by disease or accident or other misfortune, a few steps across a room may provide a true test of will and determination. Most of us require something in between.

Imagine yourself sitting at your desk at work. You're drafting a letter, and you decide you've taken a wrong turn, so you need to start over. You take the sheet of paper and crumple it into a ball, and you notice the wastepaper basket is on the other side of the room. Do you get up, walk over to it, and drop the paper quietly in? Not likely. You steady yourself, take aim, and toss the ball at the target, imagining it to be a basketball hoop or a football receiver in full stride. And when it goes in, you feel a tingling warmth that is yours alone.

That's the object of any game of skill: to provoke that feeling of *Yes!* Archery, darts, billiards, horseshoes — all of these games involve propelling an object through space at a target. All provide a sense of satisfaction when the object hits home; When *"I shot an arrow into the air/It fell to earth I know not where,"* I may have enjoyed observing its soaring flight but I exercised no control or dominion over it after it was launched. It could not respond to my will, because I exercised no will over its path. But when the object does just what I intend it to do, then I feel powerful and in control. Master of my domain.

But there are some tricky calibrations required to get the feeling just right. If the wastebasket is two feet away from me, I'll feel like an idiot if I miss, but I won't get much satisfaction out of success. If the basket is far away, but it's the size of a beer can, my chances of success are so slim that I probably won't bother trying the toss. (My chances of winning the lottery are similarly slim, but at least then the payoff is large enough to make the frequent failures tolerable.) If the archery target were as close as a dartboard, or a horseshoe stake as far away as a golf hole... you get the idea. For a game to be satisfying, it must involve enough difficulties that you feel good about overcoming them, but not so many that you can't imagine succeeding. The challenge must be appropriate for the addiction to take hold and consume us.

Golf is a game of overcoming challenges. Many of them are internal: We have to consider what kind of shot we want to hit, select the appropriate club, make the swing we've learned through repetition, and start the strategic process all over again once we've reached the point where the ball has stopped. We also have to set aside whatever psychological concerns might get in our way: our fear of failure, our nervous excitement at crucial moments, our doubt in our abilities, our overconfidence that leads to imprudent decisions. But more of them are external: water hazards, sand bunkers, long rough, trees, elevated greens, tricky putting contours, and the sheer distance from tee to green. For every golfer, there's an ideal mix of difficulties and opportunities that will provide the internal tingling warmth of knowing you overcame the obstacles and did what you set out to do.

It's the job of the course designer to provide those difficulties, ideally a host of options that allow a hard way home for the highly-skilled player and a safer route that requires more strokes but lets the lesser player complete the hole without shame. It's the job of the professional to teach the player how to swing effectively. It's the job of the equipment manufacturer to create implements that allow the player to enjoy the game. And it's the job of the governing bodies to maintain and protect the challenge of the game, making sure that it neither becomes so easy that we quit because of boredom nor so difficult that success by our own measure is hopelessly out of reach.

The player has the easy job. There's a ball in front of you. Just hit it!

Consider, however, the experience that awaits the golfer visiting one of our hypermodern "golf facilities" for the first time.

He drives his car through the gates of a community that takes its name from the golf course (itself named for some geographical feature or vegetation native to a land far away from this particular location).

Signs direct him to the parking valet who takes his keys, opens the trunk and removes his golf clubs, pockets a tip, and points him in the direction of the pro shop. He signs in, handing over a credit card and paying a figure equal to the rent on his first home. He walks out to a line of carts, one of which holds his clubs, which were whisked to the pro shop while his car was whisked into the valet lot. He follows the yellow line to the driving range, where he meets his companions and takes a few dozen swings while trying to contain his nervousness. He is called to the first tee, and he drives to where the starter awaits the group with instructions on where not to drive the cart (on the grass at all, if he's really unlucky), tells him the number of the day's pin position, and turns on the little computerized screen in the cart that displays the course's Global Positioning System information. He drives the cart along the ribbon of asphalt to the first tee box, where he has to decide which set of tees to play: the ones where he has a chance of enjoying his game or the one where his playing partners are waiting (because that's where real men play from). Not wanting to make a bad impression, he goes along.

The course — built on land chosen not for its qualities for golf but because it's where the developer could get permits — is flat but has lots of water hazards (which look great in the real-estate brochure). To maximize the number of golf-frontage lots, each hole is lined with houses on one or both sides. The routing snakes its way through the community in a pattern familiar only to lab mice in a maze; except for the first and last holes of each nine, no hole is visible from any other hole. The flat terrain and the impossibility of walking make each shot feel like it's being played in a simulator, except that there's real water in the hazards that swallow half a dozen balls during the five-hour round. After a four-dollar hot dog at the turn and a few five-dollar beers from the friendly and attractive beverage-cart girl (plus a generous tip for being attractive and friendly), the golfer is feeling a little logy as he pulls up to the cart barn where he is greeted by someone who'll wipe his clubs, pocket another tip, and whisk them up to the front of the clubhouse. After another beer and tipping the locker room attendant just for being there — he might have swiped a brush across our hero's street shoes — he finds his way to the front of the clubhouse where his car is mysteriously waiting (one last tip for the valet who loads the clubs in the trunk). He drives away, and then a few minutes after he exits the gate of the community, he stops and asks himself, "What just happened?"

In too many places, this is what golf feels like. And this is what we have to change.

Golf really should be a simple and pleasant experience. The game began in nature, on ground intended for grazing, the grass kept at a reasonable length by the sheep who strolled over the humps and hollows. This is where we found a game and a source of inner satisfaction, be it subconscious or not.

Professional players may require and receive immaculate playing conditions, lush fairways like Berber carpets, sand of a fine and uniform consistency, greens clipped so that the ball rolls as though on glass. Course superintendents will tell you that their least-favorite tournament of the year is the Masters; golfers see the manicured perfection that is Augusta National and wonder why their local country club can't look like that.

But why should it? Does the weekend softball player expect his local field to gleam like Dodger Stadium? Do touch football players ask for their field to resemble the Rose Bowl? Do basketball players stay away from the playground when the backboards aren't glass? Only the recreational golfer seems to think his experiences should be the same as those he sees on TV.

Golf isn't just one thing. It's the eighteenth at Winged Foot under U.S. Open pressure, but it's also a few holes snuck in before sunset at your local muni. It's the putting green in Edinburgh's Princes Street Gardens and a shot muffed with a smuggled club on the moon. It's a game played in solitude and good company, an excuse to be outdoors, a reason to travel, a pastime, an obsession, a test of skill, and a chance to whack something with a stick and watch it soar.

I found myself in the west of Scotland a few years ago, and I made a visit to the Isle of Seil Golf Club. It's about ten miles south of the town of Oban, where the famed single-malt whiskey is distilled. It's not a place you'd cross an ocean to play, nor would you call weeks ahead to make a reservation. I suppose you could, but there's nobody to answer the phone; the pro shop is a 10x12 foot hut with a locked metal honesty box where you deposit your £10 in an envelope (£5 for juniors), and then off you go for as long as you wish to play. The nine-hole course, played twice around, adds up to a par 62 of 4,282 yards. The greens are hand-mown once a week, there are sheep in the fields beside the course, and found balls available from an egg carton in the clubhouse/pro shop (the hut) for 30p each or four for a pound. It's a place where your expectations melt away as you rediscover the simple pleasures of swinging a club and walking in the seaside air. It's not a place where you want to drag out your Biggest Big R7-983 Bigfoot; you almost wish you had hickory shafts and hand-hammered irons to play with. Your score means nothing, except as compared to what you shot the day before over the same ground.

Come with me and let's try to reconnect with the values of the game. Let's explore why we play, consider what satisfies us, enjoy the charm of selecting equipment and the anticipation that our belief in magic conjures. We must put aside the things we don't need and emphasize the things we do. There's a lot of joy to be found on the greensward if we remember to look for it.

CHAPTER ONE: Meta-*Fore!*

I.

Once upon a time, on a farm alongside Loch Bowegon, Farmer Tom looked over his five-acre back lot that had lain fallow for more years than he could remember. He was strong, Farmer Tom was, and swift, with legs well developed from many years of physical labor. Few in the village of Bowegon could match him when a stray wandered away from the flock; Tom took off in pursuit regardless of the distance involved, bounding easily over whatever stone walls or streams lay in his path, and once he'd found his quarry he guided it back to its home fields with a firm but gentle touch.

As Tom pondered the property, he noticed that it contained a brook that ran to the loch, some randomly piled rocks from a clearing project long cast aside, and a few heaps of thatch. In the late afternoons, to keep in shape he took to walking or even jogging through these disorderly acres, not idly but deliberately putting himself before these impediments and making himself find a way over and through them.

One day his neighbor Jock joined him for his perambulations, and Jock noticed that Tom's frequent transits had worn a light path through the grasses. The track reminded Jock of the cross-country runs of his youth, when he was champion harrier of the Greater Bowegon Area. Jock asked Tom if he had tried running through the field; Tom laughed and replied that his days of running for its own sake were behind him, but Jock was welcome to if he wished. Jock nodded his thanks and took off at a comfortable clip, careful to avoid the brambles along the fringes of the path, but diligent about surmounting the obstacles that Tom had confronted along his way.

When he returned to where Tom was waiting, Jock found that he was surprisingly pleased with the feeling the run had given him. He not only enjoyed it, but he knew he wanted to do it again; he had stumbled a little coming over the brook and was sure he could do better in clearing the low stone wall near the corner of the property. Next time he will surely do better, he thought to himself.

The next time he went to visit Tom, he asked again if he could try to run the path, and he did do better at the stone wall and the brook, though he found new difficulties in keeping his footing as he careened over the mounds he'd given no thought to before. Tom was pleased to see the satisfaction Jock took in his physical exertions, and he told Jock he was welcome to come to the property any time he wished to use it.

Jock returned frequently to run what he called "the course," and before long Tom noticed that Jock was bringing a stopwatch along so he could time himself on his rounds. There were also some new worn spots at the approaches to some of the natural hurdles; Jock had observed that a slight rise a few steps off the trodden path enabled him to glide atop and over the stone wall without slowing to leap and recover, and the other hazards had better angles of attack than the straight line Tom had paced as well. Jock was applying his mental skills as well as his physical ones to the task of completing the course as expeditiously as possible. When he did improve upon his previous times, he felt great satisfaction; when he didn't, he resolved to return and do better.

Where Tom had seen a physical and mental challenge, Jock found a game.

II.

Other residents of Greater Bowegon saw Jock engaged in his new pastime and thought it looked like something they might want to try. They approached Tom for permission, and he gave it gladly, but soon there were so many taking part that the participants were getting in each other's way. These new runners turned to Jock for guidance in getting around the course and started to compete with him for the fastest times and the fewest slips and blunders. Jock understood the impulse they all felt to get out there, both for the pleasure of the endeavor and the personal challenge of testing their abilities and limits against an objective standard. But Jock missed the quiet mornings he used to spend in solitude in the field; some days there were so many wanting to use Tom's land that he had to wait in line for the chance to get started.

Jock decided to create a place of his own where he could make his run whenever he pleased, with or against his selected friends. The only land he had available was flat and dull, with none of the rocks and streams and thatch that had drawn Tom to the course in the first place. But Jock was resourceful, and he'd run the course often enough to have an idea of how to make it interesting. He dug trenches to replace the brook he loved to leap over; he lined up sawhorses to simulate the stone wall; he hauled rocks in from other parts of the property; he lay down timber in piles to be clambered over. If you looked at the field from a distance, it looked odd: a rectangular piece of property with bits of excavation and piles of construction detritus strewn randomly around it. But if you looked closely, you could see that Jock had also run a string line that connected the starting point to all the obstacles in a pattern that ran out, across, around, and back, confronting him with each blockage once per circuit.

To the casual observer, Jock's morning runs looked like the product of a mind adrift: Why was he going directly towards and over that big pile of wood, leaping over that ditch, bouncing atop those planks when he could so easily run around and avoid them? Jock's field may have lacked the bushes that made the roundabout route a necessity on Tom's, but he was able to recreate the experience by laying out a rambling path despite the open ground.

Once Jock showed the neighbors that you could create the conditions of Tom's field by building artificial obstacles, they begged him to build courses on their own unpromising land. There were soon a dozen courses in the area, then hundreds around the country. People everywhere wanted to compete with themselves and, soon, with each other. In each village the courses were a bit different — some with ponds and rivers you had to cross, others with tunnels you had to crawl through — and those who participated developed different skills to cope with the local conditions.

The activity took on a name — obstak — and each town with a course held competitions to determine the fastest obstakkers. The varying conditions meant that the champion at one field might not be among the best ten or twenty at another. With so many people getting involved, a cry rang out to set up formal rules and regulations, so that a national championship, open to all, could be held in a manner that was fair to all comers.

While Jock and all the rest of the obstakkers concentrated on preparing for the competition on their specially built obstak courses,

Tom went back to his callisthenic endeavors through and around his rolling lot, now abandoned by those who'd flocked to run its paths. He enjoyed the solitude of this personal time and took special pleasure as the natural contours reestablished themselves after all the pounding they had absorbed.

III.

The game of obstak grew steadily, as people found themselves attracted to it for reasons they could not quite explain. This lack of understanding had no effect on the game's popularity. They came to play over and over again. They played in groups and by themselves, testing their skills and competing with friends.

As time went on and villagers moved out into the wider world, they took obstak with them, developing their own courses based on what they remembered about their days running through the fields of Loch Bowegon. There was an ever-growing need for new obstak courses, and those obstakkers who were most proficient or just seemed to love the game the most were entrusted with laying out these new fields. In time this became a respected profession. They used their artistic flair and talent to design around whatever the land presented. The earliest designers, unable to move much dirt or change the landscape, created very natural-looking courses; later creators took advantage of new equipment to mold the land to their desires. Some of their efforts were hailed for being modern, but others flaunted their artificiality, with parkland features dropped into courses in the desert, and inland tree-linings used amongst the sand dunes on the shore. The best designers managed to build courses that looked less like they were invented and more like they were discovered.

Some of the courses had many water features the obstakkers had to overcome. Others were very hilly; some were dead flat. Each, however, had its own personality built into it, a signature of its designers who became much sought-after and famous. Too famous in some cases, as the most celebrated builders became quickly overcommitted and merely lent their names to courses created entirely by apprentices. They justified this by pointing to the "schools" associated with some Renaissance painters, who may not have applied all the brushstrokes themselves. They argued that their assistants were carefully trained in their own signature principles, and indeed those who engaged the designers knew what they were getting and rarely complained. The famous names would forever adorn these new courses, and the great designers always appeared at the opening and shook hands with everyone who came to see them. They were popular, and obstak was spreading, and there was lots of money to be made at it.

IV.

Why do we play games? What are we hoping to get out of them? What purpose do they serve?

There are eight reasons we might play a game:

(1) To pass the time.

(2) For pure physical or mental pleasure.

(3) For social interaction.

(4) For exercise.

(5) To learn something.

(6) To escape.

(7) To demonstrate dominance over an opponent.

(8) To measure ourselves.

For some people, to whom stillness and quiet are excruciating, simple games — or complicated games — can occupy an otherwise restless mind. Games that pass the time (1) are a staple of little kids on long car trips and adult intellectuals: license plate bingo or I-Spy for the younger set, crossword puzzles and sudoku for the older group. Mental stimulation (2) is a part of almost any game that involves strategy, be it chess, bridge, tennis, or tic-tac-toe; some may find pure pleasure in the physical acts that are part of a game — a well-stroked forehand drive, running to catch a ball in the air, a crisply-struck 5-iron — but those sensations are also available in practice or in non-game activities like tai chi or yoga. Games can provide an excuse for social gatherings (3), a pleasant time on a golf course with friends, rotating doubles at a tennis club, a party thrown where everyone plays charades. Tennis, basketball, volleyball, soccer can all provide outlets for exercise (4), especially for those who prefer to have their workouts spiced with the stimulation (2) that comes with a game. Many games provide an opportunity to learn something external (5), whether it's unimportant facts (Trivial Pursuit) or behavior and history (Diplomacy, Risk). Nearly all games help a player to escape his everyday life for as long as he concentrates on it (6), but in some games (Dungeons & Dragons) the fantasy escape is the point of playing, providing the opportunity to occupy an entirely different persona. And an important motivation for some of the most serious game players (especially men) is the establishment of dominance (7), the desire not merely to show competence but to crush an opponent — killer instinct being the mark of a champion, whether his name is Tiger Woods or Gary Kasparov.

But few games allow us to measure ourselves (8), either against an objective standard or against our own past efforts. Those games are precious opportunities to take stock, to learn, and to grow, as long as we accept full responsibility for our performances.

V.

Many obstakkers enjoyed the game so much that they found they spent most of their time at the course, challenging others and finding that with a little wager here and there they could make enough to support themselves without other work. It was not an extravagant living, but it was good enough, and certainly enjoyable, and more lucrative than anything else they knew how to do.

Those who saw obstak as a hobby, an avocation, or a diversion did not look kindly upon these full-time obstakkers, or FTOs. They were derided as "obstak bums," and the part-timers (PTOs) resented the advantage that the FTOs seemed to have when on their favorite courses. FTOs were winning almost all of their matches against the PTOs, and a cry went up to create some lines of division between the two groups.

With their income eroding because of their evident superiority — only the most foolhardy would wager against them — the FTOs discovered that they could smooth things over with the PTOs by taking them around the courses and giving them pointers on how best to surmount the hurdles, how to run the corners more efficiently, how to improve their skills and practice habits. The FTOs also became the prime distributors of specialized footwear and clothing for obstakkers.

Amongst themselves, the FTOs organized formal competitions that proved popular spectator events; they charged admission, which generated a prize-money pool for the top performers. The part-timers in turn arranged competitions that excluded all FTOs, defined as those who earned a living from obstak. PTO competitions were conducted with the amiable spirit of the individual and personal sport it had originally been, a diversion for gentlemen who competed for the pure sake of the pleasure of the sport. On the local level, clubs were formed by those who liked to play together, most clubs creating their own courses and sponsoring championships for their members and engaging brother clubs in friendly competitions. These clubs became highly organized, with officers and constitutions and codes of etiquette that reflected their members' desire to limit the activities of the full-time professionals.

VI.

Most organizations come into existence because of a need. For obstakkers, it was the desire to determine a true national champion.

A number of wealthy individuals who'd met through their clubs' friendly competitions decided to hold a grand jamboree at which they'd determine who was the fastest and best of them all and crown him their champion. In their insularity, they were certain that they'd personally seen all the serious contenders for the title. A champion was crowned, but they then learned that at a different location an assembly of obstakkers unknown to them had staged their own tournament and hailed their own so-called "national champion."

This situation could not stand, and so representatives from some of the older and more prestigious obstak courses convened to deal with the challenge. They drew up a charter and formed an organization to administer the game. It was called the United States Obstak Association (USOA), a single entity that would have the power to formalize the rules and make decisions in the best interests of the game itself. The USOA would stage a championship that was open to all, as well as one for PTOs only, and these separate national champions, representing different constituencies and levels of the sport, would be accepted by all who played the game.

After the USOA was formed, and not to be outdone, the world colonizers also gathered together representatives from the older, established clubs, but rather than forming a separate unit, they designated (as though by divine right) one single club to be the custodian of the game in their domain — which they considered to be all the world save that one-time colony known as the USA. The Royal Obstak Club of St. Drews (ROC) took on this responsibility, considering itself the rightful heir of the landholders of nearby Loch Bowegon and thus the home of the game.

The USOA and ROC had the true spirit of the game at heart, and in the early stages of incorporation they understood exactly what it was they were trying to protect. This principle was vaguely outlined but never precisely delineated, as questions arose on a case-by-case basis. The decisions rendered set precedent, and the Book of Precedents grew thick until it came to embody the essence of the game itself. There were three main principles of obstak, understood by those who created and popularized the game: run the course as you find it; your results are yours and yours alone; do no harm to the game or those who play it. These wise statements appeared nowhere in the Book, though clearly they were what guided the early decisions. The rules makers imagined that everyone knew what they meant when they banned a technique or piece of equipment for "not being traditional or customary." In time, however, decisions were being made by those who had learned the Precedents but were far removed from the founding principles themselves.

The game was being enjoyed by so many that some situations arose that were not anticipated by the original rules makers. What happens if your opponent topples the hurdle you are about to jump? How many seconds' penalty is he given for this? May an obstakker carry a stick that he uses to steady himself if he starts to fall? What if two competitors' sticks collide? May a competitor use his stick to knock his opponent's stick out of his way? These and many other issues were pondered, and decisions were rendered that permitted a runner to bring with him whatever he could carry — the carrying was considered penalty enough — but not to use it to impede anyone else. This led to questions of intent and interpretation, and so referees were assigned to the most important matches, and championship committees formed to train and oversee the referees and select the courses on which matches would be held. Another committee was formed to decide at what point a part-time obstakker became an official FTO, as the divide in terms of skill was growing greater all the time, and the split between their championship levels was becoming increasingly entrenched, though the rules that governed them remained the same.

With decisions being made on precedent alone, without reference to guiding principles, the deciders increasingly based their rulings on convenience and benefit to the organizations themselves. The spirit of the game may not have been unknown to them, but it was not their primary guide. Obstak entered into the age of bureaucrats and lawyers.

The thorniest issues arose in the area of equipment for the game. Crude walking sticks for balance had seemed an unimportant addition when they were first hacked from tree limbs and carried by hand. Farmer Tom himself had often brought one with him on his excursions over his Loch Bowegon field. But in time they gave way to rods of steel and then fiberglass that were used as vaulting poles to help clear the taller hurdles, sending the obstakker flying over stone walls his predecessors had had to run along. Having allowed sticks in the first place, the USOA and ROC did not feel they could bar the use of such poles simply on the basis of their composition.

With this door opened, the road to ruin stood beckoningly in the distance.

VII.

When we play golf, we are engaged in as pure and simple a game as the mind of man has devised. For all the trappings we've worked into it — for all the manicured greens and sculpted bunkers and space-age materials and GPS/laser distance-measuring systems — all the game requires is that we place a ball at a designated Point A, strike it with a club, and keep doing so until it comes to rest at the designated Point B.

Even if the game is played in the company of others, we play it alone. No one is propelling a ball towards us; it sits motionless on the ground. We have no need to play defense; no opponent will smash it past us into an unplayable position. Nothing that anyone else does will affect our situation: If someone else's ball happens to strike ours, we return it to its original place. Our attitude is active, not reactive. The ball waits for us to initiate the play, travels over and along the landscape, comes to rest, and waits for us to start again.

Except in foursomes — alternate shot — we have no teammates to help us out or let us down, and no opponent can deprive us of our chances. Our score, our total of the number of times we struck at the ball between Points A and B, is ours alone. It was ours yesterday, and it is ours today, and it will be ours tomorrow.

We are responsible for our good shots and can take pride in them. We are responsible for our bad shots and must accept their consequences. The Rules forgive us some of our worst trespasses — they don't demand that we play underwater, and they permit us in our sole discretion to declare a predicament impossible — but they extract a penalty for our doing so.

Every round of golf asks us the question, Who are we today? Nothing we did yesterday provides answers. Nothing we'll learn to do tomorrow can aid us. All we have is today's number, today's total. The only shot that matters is the next one.

Because of this — because of all of this — golf is the most ruthlessly efficient way of measuring ourselves in the form of a game that we will ever encounter. And because of that, it is the most valuable and precious game we can play. This is why we play it, whether we realize it or not.

VIII.

Obstak had become an international craze. Courses sprang up throughout the landscape, and real-estate developers soon planned whole communities around the amenity offered by obstak clubs. The courses themselves were pleasant parklike surroundings to walk through even for those who did not play: The majority of the residents enjoyed sitting on their porches looking at a wonderfully manicured lawn that they didn't have to maintain (until all the houses were sold and the course and its maintenance budgets were ceded to them), watching the obstakkers do their thing.

Even around the best-known of the old-line obstak courses — those on which great events had been held in the past and which had provided fair tests for the most skilled and famous of the FTOs — houses sprang up, and the value of the properties soared when owners realized they could rent out their homes for exorbitant prices when the FTOs came to town for the national championships. The FTOs themselves had gone from being highly skilled locals who eked out a living advising their less-talented brethren, to nomads who were treated like visiting sultans as they traveled the world and competed in high-paying competitions amongst the demonstrated elite of the game. They came to expect the best of everything and some grumbled when a competition course was not to their liking or when they were obliged to spend their valuable time jogging around the courses and giving pointers to the sponsors and businessmen who had put up the tournament purse and whose love for the game made the professionals' livelihood possible.

Some of the courses selected by the USOA and ROC for its championships became as famous as the most famous Obstakkers themselves. PTOs would plan trips to these far-flung locations, and would talk for years about what they'd done when they faced the hazards they'd seen on TV. Courses came to be prized for their difficulty, boosting the ego of the designer who created the most difficult course. The more they tested the FTOs, the more determined the less-skilled players became to see how they faired with their less-developed abilities on them or just to brag that they played such a course "from the tips." This was true even though they rarely enjoyed the actual experience; there was something manly about facing the same hurdles as the big boys, even if the final results were predictable and never mentioned.

To help the part-timers — who could only jump three feet in the air on average – over a six-foot obstacle built for the FTOs, designers built stairs to a three-foot-high platform placed alongside the hurdle, and extended peninsulas into the takeoff areas for the water jumps. Such modifications somehow kept the average obstakker from recognizing the gap between his abilities and those of the pros.

The vogue for the most difficult possible course — along with the modifications and aids that would let the ordinary player complete the course in one piece, never mind doing so competitively — led course designers to create ever longer, tougher, and more unpleasant layouts. Members of the clubs that regularly used these courses were proud of having a place that would challenge the most able FTO, even as their muscles ached and bones were broken in their attempts to do things beyond their abilities. In an unguarded moment they might acknowledge that they were happier when their courses were more in line with their abilities, but they only said this when they were amongst themselves. "A good members' course" was a phrase used condescendingly, in comparison to "a championship course," even though no championships would ever be held on the places that gave themselves that name.

As the elite obstakkers got faster and stronger and leapt higher and farther, the USOA grew concerned about the situation. At its events it made the hurdles even higher and the jumps longer and the corners tighter to try to force the FTOs to slow down. But the professionals had access to the newest equipment, and their aerodynamically designed clothes and springlike shoes with wider-ridged soles for better cornering and their ever more efficient vaulting poles kept pace with the USOA's efforts. "This new equipment must be abolished, or the game will suffer," declared the USOA, even though the vast majority of participants needed all the help they could get just to make it around the souped-up courses. The game was becoming so difficult that beginners came away from their initial efforts feeling humiliated, despite the special mounds and platforms and peninsulas set up for their benefit. Few returned for a second taste.

The USOA and ROC formed committees to review the game's equipment. They knew the game was being spoiled, and they could see it in the fast times being turned in at the top levels of competition. Rather than concentrating on designing special challenges for their championships, which attracted less than one percent of all who play the game, they decided to crack down on the manufacturers. The shoes with springs in them had to go; so did the wider-soled footwear and the improved vaulting poles.

The Book of Precedents said that equipment had to be "in the traditions of the game," and that was clear enough to those who'd long played the game. But lawyers for the equipment-makers argued in court that since the helpful developments had been permitted for several years, they had become traditions of their own. The courts disagreed, but fighting the lawsuit would potentially drain the treasury of the USOA, and with the legal system now being asked to judge what was traditional in obstak, more suits would surely follow.

The governing committees decided they needed a clear set of standards. But clarity was elusive. Rubber-soled shoes have a certain bounciness to them; how much is too much? Where does resiliency end and improper springing begin? With no stomach for fighting the manufacturers, the USOA set a limit that was higher than any existing or planned shoe could deliver. While the courts had agreed that the organization could prevent any springlike effect in the shoes, their own new rules allowed a certain amount of springing. The ROC went even further, setting standards that were more lax than the USOA's. The manufacturers cried foul, proclaimed that the petty rules makers were taking the best technology out of the hands of the average obstakker — claims that were mostly hype to begin with — but they knew what the new standards meant: Their lawsuits had served their intention, which was to intimidate the ruling bodies into letting them do as they wished.

The game of obstak was now in the hands of those who profited from it, rather than those who played and loved it.

IX.

The game of golf is at a crossroads. The people who govern it have forgotten what the game is about. They have focused their attention on the elite few who play in championships at the national level and are writing rules to keep the best players from making it seem too easy. But is it too easy in most people's experience? Does anyone know of anybody who has given up the game because it's too easy?

"They're hitting the ball too far!" we hear over and over. "The great courses of the past will be obsolete! We have to rein in the ball, limit the clubs, build our courses longer and longer, or the game we love will disappear."

Does the following sound familiar? "Our longest holes are little more than a drive and a putt. My feeling is that if the game continues to improve in the matter of its length and we get just a little more resiliency in the ball and a little better clubs than we have now, the game in [the] future will be relegated to the only place where it can be played, and that is on the great prairies of our Western country." The orotund language at the end may give it away, but it's still startling to realize that this concern was expressed by the USGA President, R. H. Robertson, in 1902. *Golf Illustrated* added its opinion in 1910: "If the carrying power of golf balls is to be still further increased, all our golf courses will be irretrievably ruined as a test of the game." Either distance has always and will always be a problem, or it has always been overstated as a problem, with each generation forgetting the effect its younger efforts had on the generation before it.

For the professionals, the game has changed in the last twenty years, thanks to some foolish decisions about equipment, advances in agronomy, a radical change in players' workout ethic, and advanced motion analysis. Taking those four points in reverse order:

Advanced Motion Analysis: Thanks to the modern computer revolution, we are no longer guessing when we try to improve a player's swing We know the optimal launch conditions for every swing speed, and through video analysis and equipment fitting can help a player reach those conditions in a repeatable fashion.

Players' Workouts: Before Tiger Woods came on the scene, it was noteworthy when a pro golfer had any workout program at all, unless he was recovering from an injury. Gary Player and few others were advocates for physical fitness; their fellow professionals thought they were "health nuts." Tiger demonstrated the value of strength and flexibility, and golfers across the PGA Tour realized they had to improve their physical conditioning if they hoped to compete. Today, the rotund and flabby bodies are the exceptions, and rarely is the question asked whether golfers are athletes.

Agronomy: With new strains of grass that will tolerate tighter and tighter mowing without dying, fairways have been made firmer and faster than ever before — nearly as fast as the greens of a generation ago — and this has contributed to perfect conditions and (mildly) to the increases in distance.

Equipment: The biggest difference in the game is in the equipment. Twenty-plus years ago, players were using persimmon woods to hit wound balata balls; today they use titanium trampoline-faced drivers to propel solid multilayered and urethane-covered balls that have been formulated to react differently when hit with different clubs.

The rules governing equipment stated clearly that the face of a club could not have the effect of a spring. In the next few chapters, we'll examine just how manufacturers came to develop a driver that has an effect that is contrary to the literal interpretation of the rules. What we cannot explain is why the ruling bodies allowed them into the game, except that they were afraid of lawsuits and thus opened the barn door wide and waved the horse away.

Regardless, why should we be surprised when golfers today hit the ball farther than they did years ago? Sprinters run faster than they did years ago; weightlifters hoist more kilos than they used to; high and long jumpers cover more air and ground. Improvements in training and nutrition guarantee that athletes will keep getting better. Golf is not immune.

The worry would be unimportant if it weren't for its ripple effects. In the name of adjusting for the world of the top 0.5 percent performers, those who would make money from our love of the game are making our experience of it worse.

Because of the hue and cry over equipment, developers and designers feel they must stretch their courses far beyond the distance that the average avid golfer wishes to play. (I have conducted a worldwide survey confirming that fewer than one-fifth of all male golfers prefer to play courses longer than 6,600 yards.) This requires more land and more maintenance and drives up the price of a round of golf. This fear also induces designers to make their courses more difficult, and these courses take longer to play, further reducing the players' pleasure in the game. And all of this concern has NOTHING to do with the game as played by the overwhelming majority of golfers.

We have to stop obsessing about how far the pros can hit the ball. We have to demand and choose courses that reflect our game, with no concern about the 500–900 extra yards that we don't want to play anyway. We have to understand what we want and love about our own imperfect efforts, and we have to embrace those things that celebrate them and reject those that interfere with our enjoyment. It's our game, not the professionals', and we should only accept those changes that serve our needs.

CHAPTER TWO: Implements

One important thing to realize about golf is that it is a very mature game.

I don't mean that those who play it are mature, or even aged; I've observed too many hurled clubs and epithets to believe anything so foolish. I mean that it has been in existence for a very long time, long enough for the process of trial and error to have worked its merciless logic on all innovations and breakthroughs. When you think about golf equipment — and I've spent much of my adult life thinking about golf equipment — you're pondering a centuries-old process of evolution in which the fittest ideas survive and the rest fall away.

True innovations come into being for a reason and are accepted with remarkable speed. When Gene Sarazen soldered a flange onto a lofted iron to give it bounce and invented the modern sand wedge, unveiling it at the 1932 British Open, he changed bunker play almost overnight, as his competitors quickly copied the idea and manufacturers followed suit. When Titleist introduced the solid-core multilayered Pro V1 in 2000, the wound ball — an evolving technology that had defined state-of-the-art for more than a century — largely disappeared from the pro tours in a matter of weeks.

Golf balls have dimples not because of a brilliant theoretical discovery, but because of a combination of serendipity and the powers of observation. When gutta-percha balls, shaped from the rubbery resin of the namesake tree, replaced sewn pouches stuffed with feathers as the ball of choice, players noticed that these balls flew farther after they had been used for a while and acquired some surface nicks and scrapes. These unintentional imperfections combine with the ball's backspin to create a turbulent layer of air around it in flight, reducing the aerodynamic drag forces and increasing the lift forces as it travels, thus staying aloft longer than a smooth sphere would. No one thought this up and used the idea to launch a product line; golfers and ball makers saw the effects and then deliberately put impressions on the outside of the ball. Through trial and error involving variously shaped and spaced patterns of indentations, an approximately ideal form of roughness became standard. This pattern has changed very little in the last hundred years, with only a very minor bit of tweaking to optimize the effect.

When you consider new technologies and equipment, the essential question is, Does this innovation serve a recognizable purpose? If so, it will last. If not, or if the purpose is minor or insignificant, it's not worth attending to.

Golf is a game defined by its equipment. Rule 1-1 states, "The Game of Golf consists of playing *a ball* with *a club* from the teeing ground into the hole by a stroke or successive strokes in accordance with the Rules" [emphasis added]. The three necessary elements are a ball, a club, and a hole. If you throw a ball at a target, if you hit a ball at a distant plank, if you club a disk towards a goal, you're playing a game but you're not playing golf.

Historians tracing the creation of our game look to the equipment to distinguish golf from stick-and-ball games that might be related. Since games were generally not the subject of close written histories in the midmillennium, we can only speculate on the basis of paintings that have survived and draw inference from the implements shown and the placement of the participants at play.

Golf is distinct from pall-mall, a game played in the 16ᵗʰ and 17ᵗʰ centuries and a precursor to croquet, since the large wooden ball in that game was struck with a mallet towards a distant hoop. The name pall mall or *pallemaille*. comes from the Italian *pallamaglio*, which literally means "ball-mallet." The straight-line alleys that served as courses for this game grew into curveless roads or promenades like those in London that bear names reflecting this evolution (Pall Mall, the Mall). Others developed into popular shopping concourses similar to those associated with the word "mall" today.

The Dutch game of *kolven* involved propelling a heavy wooden ball towards target poles, but the early depictions of the game — played in an enclosed court or on open ice — suggest that the ball was pushed by the large-headed sticks in a manner similar to a hockey wrist shot, rather than swung at in a golfing stroke. The Flemish game *chole* may have been the closest ancestor, with an iron-headed club used to strike a ball towards a chosen target (a door, a designated part of a wall), but the game — still played in parts of northern France and Belgium — includes an aspect of defense, as one side takes a specified number of strokes, and then the opposing side gets one shot with which to propel the ball away from the end point.

The modern golfer with his surgically precise instruments identified by number is often amused and confused by the array of names given to older clubs: play-club, brassie, baffing spoon, mashie, niblick. In order to make sense of the clubs of a prior generation, it is necessary to understand that each was developed to serve a purpose. In parallel with the evolution of the ball, the clubs tell us the story of how golf grew.

Before considering early equipment, we have to put aside all of our notions of golf's field of play. Rule 1-1 says nothing about a fairway or rough or hazards or putting greens. (The teeing ground is mentioned, but only because a game needs a starting point as well as an object.) Golf was played on common land, not an area set aside and groomed specifically for the purpose.

The oldest surviving rules of golf, those set down in 1744 by the Gentlemen Golfers of Leith (later known as the Honourable Company of Edinburgh Golfers), begin by dictating that "(y)ou must tee your ball within a club's length of the hole." That hole was dug roughly in the ground, and since the implement we call a tee today was still 150 years in the future, the teeing of the ball consisted of either kicking up a tuft of turf on which to prop your ball for the initial shot or making a small mound with dirt most likely drawn from the previous hole. All that commotion took place right beside the hole — and we get upset when there's a spike mark in our path!

So the putting surface wasn't exactly pristine; then again, the ball, originally made of wood, was only as approximately round as the maker's eye allowed. It was expected to bounce and jounce along the terrain more than to soar through the sky. The initial clubs had long faces made of wood, to provide a margin of error for players striking the ball from uneven ground.

When the game began, golfers probably set out with just one club, but the nature of the playing field soon led to some specialized adaptations. Balls could land in muddy areas or among brambles and stones; there were ruts caused by wagon wheels, and if your ball got stuck in one of those you could not reasonably hit it with a long-nosed wood. Since no one expected perfect conditions, no one expected relief from imperfect spots; if you hit it there, you had to play from there. (The game was almost exclusively match play, so a high number only cost you one hole.) For these shots, golfers turned to the blacksmith or forge to create short-nosed clubs with iron heads. To help loft the ball into the air when faced with difficult conditions between yourself and the hole, wooden heads were made with concave faces; these "spoons" scooped the ball over the intervening trouble. The golfer was not expected to solve all problems with a single tool; as early as 1502, when James IV of Scotland placed an order with a bowmaker in Perth, it was for a set of clubs.

The oldest surviving clubs are on display at Royal Troon, and may have been created in the 1600s, or even earlier. There are six woods — play-clubs, as what we'd call "drivers" were termed, and spoons — and two irons, a heavy iron and a light iron. Both irons have truncated squared-off faces; the heavy iron has a "spur" at the bottom of the toe to help extract the ball from particularly ticklish spots. The shafts are much longer than we are used to, and this combined with the lie of the heads tell us that the model swing was a flat one, taken from a distance, more like a hockey slap shot than a modern golfer's swing.

Over the next two hundred years, clubs changed very little, and the conditions of the course changed hardly at all. Links were laid out where the ground allowed, and those who'd been using the land for their other recreation just kept on doing so. For a contemporary equivalent, think of the way some public parks have "Frisbee golf" courses over spaces used at the same time by family picnickers.

When membership clubs were formed in the 18th century, they were not clubs in the American style, not groups owning real estate over which the game is played. They met to hold competitions and to eat and drink in chosen company. Their golf was no different from that of their townsmen and -women, and they had no special claim of privileges on the links.

Towards the middle of the 19th century, it became more common for land to be set aside for the purpose of playing golf. We are still a long way away from manicured conditions, however. The putting areas looked no different from the rest of "the green" (meaning the whole playing area; the word lives on in the phrase "through the green," which even today is defined as all areas of the golf course except the putting surfaces, teeing ground, and hazards — it's the sense of the word that gives us green fees and greenkeepers), but they were granted a bit of relief from being the teeing area as well: the 1812 rules of St. Andrews set the teeing distances as between two and four club-lengths from the previous hole, and by 1875 this had been extended to 8 to 12 club-lengths. An 1815 code from Aberdeen defines the putting area as 15 yards from the hole in all directions and permits the removal of loose impediments in this designated area; in 1829 the golfers of St. Andrews extended that definition to 20 yards, and that held sway until the 1950s.

The next significant change came with the development in 1845 of a new kind of ball, shaped in a single piece from the resin of the gutta-percha tree. This rubberlike solid ball was heavier and did not go quite as far as the feathery, but it most other respects it was a boon to the game. The making of a feathery was time-consuming and labor-intensive — the most experienced ball makers could not produce as many as eight in a day — and so the cost of balls was a significant expense for those considering taking up the game. Gutties required boiling and shaping, not painstaking stuffing by hand. Moreover, if a guttie broke — as they were prone to do — it was a simple matter to gather the pieces, put them back in the boiling pot and form the ball anew. This improved technology helped bring the cost of the game within reach of a wider group and played a role in its expanding popularity. (Imagine that: a breakthrough in equipment that cost less than its predecessors!)

The guttie also had an effect on how the game was played. The sweeping stroke from a club with an extra-long shaft was not merely traditional, but had a practical side: When you hit a hand-sewn ball with a descending blow, you ran the risk of tearing the cover or increasing the stress on the seam. (The preferred method for getting featheries into the air in the equivalent of our pitch shot was a "baffing" stroke, in which the player hit the ground just behind the ball with the sole of the club and lofted it upward with the ascending clubface.) An exploded feathery was a lost ball in the truest sense of the phrase, since it was no longer a ball at all. This wasn't an issue for the guttie, and the best players began to use irons to hit approach shots to the greens, striking down on the ball to send it up into the air with greater distance control than was possible using the old technique. Allan Robertson is credited with being the first to adopt this style, which helped him become the first golfer known to have broken 80 for 18 holes on the Old Course in St. Andrews. (Irons had mostly been used for trouble shots, including the highly specialized track iron, its club face little larger than a ball, that was used to extract the ball from wheel tracks and horseshoe prints and similar tight spaces.)

With the emergence of the gutta-percha ball, players carried more iron clubs than woods for the first time. The track iron gave way to the larger-headed but lighter niblick, useful for a variety of lofted shots to and around the putting areas. Iron cleeks and mashies were used to drive the ball low with plenty of run; their shorter heads were easier to control than the wooden play-clubs and spoons, particularly when swung hard, as the denser guttie required.

The guttie changed the look of wood clubs as well; the first adaptations were still long-nosed, but they became shorter to reduce the strain on their long, slender heads, and the hitting area was growing thicker behind the face. This was not intended to increase power — though some club makers may have suggested it would, and converts no doubt claimed that the latest club gave them "20 extra yards" (the modern unit of improvement) — but to make them more durable. The ball was tough on wooden clubheads, and unlike with the feathery, it was the club that suffered the consequences.

In a quest to build more durable clubs that could better survive impact with the guttie, Thomas Johnston, an enterprising clubmaker, created a "wood" with a head made of vulcanite — a hard, resilient rubber. While this was not a notable success, it received the first patent ever granted to a golf club. Patent protection encouraged innovation, and in the last two decades of the 19th century a dizzying array of clubs and styles were devised and tried. Nearly every development in late 20th-century club making appears at this time: metal woods, offset clubs, no-hosel design, spring-faced putters, and muscleback irons were all tried, as were such now-illegal efforts as dual-faced "duplex" clubs and adjustable irons.

The changes that lasted involved none of these passing fancies. In 1888, Henry Lamb created a wood club with a much shorter head and a face that was convex rather than concave. The term "spoon" would soon be obsolete, replaced by the word "bulger," which is what Lamb called his design, in honor of its bulging face. Lamb claimed that this new design reduced hooks and slices, and while he may not have fully understood the reason, he was correct in this.

The bulging face has little effect on a ball hit on the sweet spot, and it does not reduce sidespin — toed shots still draw, shots towards the heel still fade. But the bulge pushes such shots farther away from the target line at the start, so the sidespin can then bring it back towards the middle. With its rounder, pear-shaped profile, the bulger set the look of wood clubs for most of the next hundred years.

Meanwhile, in America, Coburn Haskell, a Cleveland industrialist, was visiting a friend at the B.F. Goodrich plant in Akron, Ohio. He found some elastic rubber thread in a waste container and started rolling it around in his hands. He bounced the mass idly on the floor and had a sudden inspiration: Like all golfers, he was looking for a few extra yards, and he suggested to his friend that this material be used to make a golf ball. The new ball was made up of rubber windings around a solid core, wrapped in a gutta-percha cover, and it was livelier than any previous effort — so much so that while it became known as the Haskell ball in the United States, the British generally referred to them as "bounding billies." This new wound ball, brought onto the market in 1898, held sway among top players for nearly a hundred years.

As the wound ball became standard, the first major controversy over equipment took place. Australian-born Walter Travis traveled from America to England in 1904, and became the first American citizen to win the British Amateur. He did so thanks to his skill with the putter, and it was this object rather than the man who wielded it that got the most attention. Travis used a center-shafted mallet made by Arthur Knight of Schenectady, New York. Center-shafted models were not unknown in the U.K., but in the years after Travis's shocking victory with what became known as his "Schenectady putter," they were banned by the R&A, which had become the major governing body for the game in the golfing world outside the United States. It seems the R&A was not immune to the belief in magic; there was no particular evidence that center-shafted putters made bad putters into good ones, or good ones into world-beaters. The action could be considered an extended form of sour grapes on the part of the British; the USGA did not go along with this ban, and it remained a point of contention between the two organizations for some forty years. (The ban was the impetus for the first effort in the rules to govern equipment, requiring that clubs "not depart from the traditional and accepted form and make." This wording was adopted by the USGA in 1909 — though it noted that center-shafted putters were not "nontraditional" in its view — and I can't help thinking that it might have been enough if we'd stopped right there, before getting into measurements of coefficient of restitution, moment of inertia, initial velocity, head-size volume, and so on.)

A less controversial innovation changed the face of iron clubs — literally. Club makers had experimented with bumps and grooves on irons in an effort to create spin, once it was understood that the balls could tolerate the friction and the clubs could be marked without weakening them. With the Haskell ball firmly established — though its composition inside and out would go through several permutations as manufacturers sought the right combination of liveliness and stability — nearly all iron makers added scoring lines to the faces of their cleeks and mashies and niblicks, which were increasingly resembling the clubs we know. The clubs were manufactured through a drop-forging process, in which molten iron is poured into a form and then pressed into the desired shape; grooves or pimples were added later. Forging rather than hammering by hand made clubs cheaper and further enhanced the spread of the game.

By the second decade of the 20th century, golf courses were coming to look very much like what we know today. The putting surfaces were distinct from the fairways, and the teeing grounds had been moved away from the hole. (Tees — devices inserted into the ground, on which a ball sits until hit — gained popularity in the 1920s, replacing mounds of dampened sand.) These putting areas still had enough irregularities to them that putters were more lofted than those of today; there was no guarantee of a pure roll on the greens. (Bobby Jones's Calamity Jane had eight degrees of loft, compared to the ideal of four degrees for putters today; he needed this on bumpy and slow greens that would probably measure 4 feet on the Stimpmeter.) But the conditions of the game's grounds were fairly well stabilized, and especially in the United States — where golf was a relatively young game when it came under centralized regulations — courses were increasingly being built and shaped rather than being laid out onto natural pastures.

This stability was also a result of the influence of the ruling bodies. Golf was played for centuries before anyone felt the need to develop overarching rules; you hit the ball, you found it, and you hit it again. In the 18th century, as individual golf clubs were formed and staged competitions, each wrote its own rules to govern its play. In the 1890s, the oldest established clubs decided that the Royal and Ancient Golf Club of St. Andrews would set the rules and regulations through its Rules of Golf Committee. (In the U.S., the governing body was formed just seven years after the founding of the first club, and its role was clear from the start.) One of its purposes in doing so was to protect the traditions of the game, and the authority to ban unusual implements like the center-shafted putter was one way to do so.

A decision by the R&A and USGA slowed the adoption of the most significant change in early 20th century equipment, declaring in 1914 that steel shafts were contrary to the Rules. Club makers — not necessarily individual tinkerers any more, but sporting goods companies with complex machinery and factories — were concerned about the dwindling supplies of good hickory and were looking for other materials that could serve; they began by rolling out rods of steel and then boring out the center, making a shaft that was similar in weight to hickory but stronger and much easier to produce. Despite the ruling against this new development, manufacturers continued to make them and they were increasingly accepted by golfers, leading to a reversal by the USGA in 1924 of its ban of steel.

Steel shafts had a huge effect on the game. They were stronger than hickory, but also less flexible; professionals who were used to the whippiness of the wooden shaft had to adjust to make their swings less wristy, more unified. The consistency of the steel shafts also made it simpler for manufacturers to offer clubs in matched sets for the first time; instead of buying individual clubs and hoping they would have similar playing characteristics, a golfer could purchase a full complement of clubs machined and calibrated to play the same. ("A full complement" might be very full; some professionals carried as many as thirty or more clubs to cope with all conceivable conditions — a low driver, high driver, left-handed clubs for specialty shots, whatever a golfer might feel he needed. Robert Harris, a member of the Rules of Golf Committee of the R&A and chairman of its Golf Ball Sub-committee in the 1930s, attributed this to the rigidity of steel, as opposed to the more malleable hickory shafts that permitted much greater variation in the shots hit with each club. The USGA and R&A responded by imposing a fourteen-club limit in 1938 and '39 respectively.)

And so it is here that the game of golf took a deep breath, looked around, and decided that things were pretty good just as they are. I don't mean that there weren't further refinements and innovations — some worked, like Gene Sarazen's sand wedge; some worked too well, like the deep-grooved "backspin irons" that were outlawed when the first groove specifications were adopted in 1924 — but that the club, the ball, and the course entered into a lengthy period of stability that essentially continues today. There is a general consensus on what the game of golf is, what it should look like, and how its implements should perform.

In the second half of the 20th century, golf equipment became a very big business, and every new wrinkle was hailed as the dawn of a new era. Three of these innovations did prove to be worth the words expended on their behalf; we'll look at those in the next chapter. For the overwhelming majority of golfers, they represent the most important things you need to know about your equipment; if you understand some of the basics, then the search for the ideal will be so much easier and allow you to sleep at night knowing that what you have is about as good as it has to be for you to play your best.

CHAPTER THREE:
Three Innovations That Changed the Game

The putter looked strange, and it made a funny sound. Johnny Miller, in his book *I Call the Shots,* recalls a man with a goatee offering one of them to him and his father when he was nine years old. "At impact, the putter emitted a loud chime like a doorbell. The man smiled and said, 'What do you think?' My dad looked like he'd just bitten into a lemon. He immediately said, 'Forget it. My kid makes everything with his little Bulls Eye, and I think we'll just stick with that.'"

The man with the goatee was not discouraged, and a few years later he introduced his first product, the 1-A, which earned the name "Ping" for its distinctive acoustic properties. An inveterate tinkerer, Karsten Solheim had taken up golf as an adult, and like so many of us, he believed that some of his difficulties with the game could be blamed on the equipment — those implements famously described as being ill-suited to the purpose of getting a ball into a hole. Unlike most of us, however, he had some thoughts about what he could do about it.

In examining his putting problems, Solheim decided that they were made worse by the blade putter's tendency to twist when it contacted the ball anywhere on the face other than the sweet spot. This twisting took an imperfect stroke and translated it into an even more imperfect putt. Considering the situation from the perspective of his training as a mechanical engineer, Solheim recognized the inertial principles at work and saw that the key to reducing the twisting effect would be to increase the moment of inertia (MOI). The way to do this was to spread the weight of the clubhead farther away from the center of the face; if more weight could be placed at the heel and toe of the putter, the head would twist more slowly on contact away from the sweet spot and the ball would not be deflected off-line as much or lose as much distance as a result of imperfect impact.

The 1-A consisted of two face plates connected at the heel and toe through two blocks to a bar containing a hosel into which the club shaft was fitted. The hollow space behind the forward plate created the ringing sound. (The quality of the sound was purest when contact was made in the center of the face — auditory feedback that would help the golfer learn when he was making a proper stroke.) Solheim is said to have created the original model using popsicle sticks and two sugar cubes.

Solheim was working for General Electric in Ithaca, New York, when he first came up with the idea but had moved to GE's operation in Palo Alto, California by the time the putter first began to gather attention (and when he showed it to Larry and Johnny Miller). He was based in Phoenix in the early 1960s as his efforts to market this newfangled putter took hold. He made himself available to the pros at the annual early-season Phoenix Open, helping them adjust the lie and loft angle of their irons and gaining a reputation for his effective clubfitting. He also got them to try his putter and many of them put it in their bags. In 1962, Solheim received a patent for the heel-toe-weighted putter head, and that same year John Barnum became the first player to win on tour using a Ping putter.

Four years later, he followed this initial creation with a more traditionally styled putter, but one that still incorporated the benefits of heel-toe weighting. The club, dubbed the "Anser," no longer featured the parallel plates, but looked more like a blade with a flange attached to its back, with a cavity carved into the center of the back of the head. The "ping" sound was gone, though the name stuck, and the Anser became the best-selling putter ever devised, adopted by professionals who won countless tournament titles with it, imitated and tweaked by nearly everybody who worked seriously in putter design in the decades that followed.

I will never forget seeing Karsten sitting in the locker room at a tour event in 1969. He was waiting for a particular pro whose name I don't recall. When another pro came by, Karsten asked him if he had seen the fellow he was waiting for; this prima donna glared at Karsten and said, "I'm not his keeper, why should I know where he is?" Karsten didn't show any irritation at this rudeness but simply waited. He had the patience and the time to invest in making his innovations known.

He worked the greens relentlessly at almost every event, showing his putters and getting the pros to try them. As far as I recall he almost never gave one away; he would ask for something in return, generally $5, which was the approximate manufacturing cost of his putter that retailed for $20 to $25. I never figured out if Karsten was just tight with his money or if he really understood the psychology of making these guys reach into their pockets. I think it was the latter; by doing so, they put a value on the product, and because of this they were less likely to just give it away in the parking lot on their way out. They'd made an investment, however small, and so they had a reason to try to make it work. His tenacity and stubbornness impressed me and made Karsten one of the most successful innovators in the game.

For all the success of Ping putters, those clubs merely paved the way for the more significant development that followed.

If moving the weight away from the center of the clubface helped keep putts on line, wouldn't it work for full shots as well? This was the conceptual breakthrough that put Ping in the forefront of club manufacturing in the late 1960s, one of the most important innovations in the history of the game from the standpoint of the average golfer.

Prior to the introduction of Ping's Karsten I irons — even before the wildly successful Ping EYE model that followed — iron clubs were invariably forged, meaning they were hammered or stamped into a slender profile with only occasional variations, usually aimed at setting more weight directly behind the hitting area. These blades were wonderful for the top-notch golfer — still are — because the professional or tournament-level amateur rarely hits the ball off-center. The even distribution of weight enables the scratch-or-plus player to work the ball readily from left to right or right to left, depending on the demands of the shot. But for the average golfer, such clubs were maddeningly difficult to hit, profoundly unforgiving of less-than-perfect contact.

Solheim had left General Electric by then and had created Karsten Manufacturing Corporation in Scottsdale, Arizona, to produce the Ping Anser putters. As he pondered the issue of iron design, he recognized that the forging process would make it difficult to mass-produce the kind of perimeter-weighting pattern he wanted his clubheads to have. Reaching back into the ancient history of metallurgy, he started working with the investment-casting process, a method that dates back to the Egyptians in the time of the Pharaohs. In investment casting, a mold is formed by depositing clay around a wax model. This is done by continually dipping the model in a slurry of clay, letting it set and dipping it again until a thick layer is built up and allowed to harden. It is then fired in a furnace to form a ceramiclike mold. The wax melted and escaped through a hole, leaving a hollow mold; you could then pour the stainless steel (or whatever metal you wanted) into the cavity, and when it cooled, the ceramic mold would be broken away, leaving a metal replica of the wax model. After this was cleaned up and polished it was assembled into a club.

The advantage of this process is the ability to create intricate designs not possible from the forging process at that time. The intricacy can be seen in gold jewelry created this way during the time of the Pharaohs or in bronze sculptures from Roman days. Or even the tooth crowns in your mouth if you've been unlucky enough to need them. (For obvious reasons, this is also known as a "lost wax" process.)

Another benefit of investment casting is that it can be used with a much wider variety of metals than forging. Forged irons were made from regular iron or steel and were prone to rusting; to make a stainless model the clubs had to be plated with chrome. But the investment molds could be filled with molten stainless steel or other alloys, and because the process is so precise — much more so than the compression forces involved in forging — the resulting product usually requires no additional machining. The "unfinished" look of a Ping clubhead — a peened look which results from tumbling the head in a barrel of stones — made it distinctive in a sea of shining chrome-plated blades.

Most distinctive, however, was the half-moon cut out of the back of the Karsten I iron. Golfers may not have understood why these clubs were more forgiving — for a detailed but simple explanation of moment of inertia, see chapter four — but they could definitely feel the difference on so-so impacts. It no doubt seemed counterintuitive to the player that he could hit more straight shots by moving weight away from the sweet spot, but his happiness at watching those shots fly truer and higher more than made up for any confusion. He may also have noticed that his hands didn't hurt quite as much on missed shots; the clubhead's resistance to twisting meant that there was slightly less stinging feedback rising to his grip to tell him he'd done something wrong.

Solheim's breakthrough was to design a club for the benefit of the average golfer. There was almost no difference between the results of a shot hit on the sweet spot of a forged blade and one hit on the sweet spot of a cavity back (as the perimeter-weighted clubs came to be known). The difference came on shots hit off the sweet spot; the perimeter weighting had the effect of expanding the functional sweet spot by making the club more forgiving when the golfer missed it.

This is also why it was not necessarily a great club for the professional. The pros don't miss the sweet spot. They also want feedback from their clubs; their sensibilities are finely tuned, and they want to be able to feel the slightest variations in quality of contact. They want to be able to subtly influence the flight of the ball through adjustments in swing plane and face presentation. They intend the flight path to be slightly off line on certain occasions, something the cavity back club resists. They want clubs that are as responsive as possible, and perimeter weighting dampens the response in ways that the handicap player doesn't normally perceive.

Nick Price once explained the difference to me like this: With perimeter-weighted clubs, considering his shots on a scale from one to ten, he knew that he wouldn't hit a shot that was worse than a six, but because of the club's resistance to subtle influences a pro wants to impart, the best shots wouldn't be better than an eight or nine. With blades, a bad shot might be as bad as a three, but the best shots would be tens — and the difference between an eight or nine and a ten on the top end was the difference between winning and losing a major championship.

For most golfers, though, Pings initiated the class of equipment now referred to as "game-improvement clubs." The casting process enabled Solheim to experiment with different shapes and weightings. The half-moon cavity on the Karsten I's became a broader almond-shaped opening on the well-named Ping EYE clubs, which then expanded further across the back in the Ping EYE2 — perhaps the most successful clubs ever marketed, an immediate hit when they were introduced in 1982.

Best of all, Karsten Manufacturing had set a high standard for the consistency of its clubs. The precision of the investment-casting process meant that there were very few bad Ping clubs being produced. Forging, which was a much more variable process, demanded close attention to every aspect of production, from the quality of the materials to the consistency of the forged part and the grinding and stamping prior to chrome plating. Even a reputable manufacturer had to accept that a certain number of "out of spec" clubs would come off the assembly line. But there were very few of these with casting, so long as the molds were properly created.

Better clubs, simpler to manufacture, easier to hit, and more forgiving — Ping's clubs were a victory for golfers everywhere and ushered in a revolution in golf equipment and the philosophy behind it that is still reverberating throughout the game four decades later.

I came to think of Karsten as a friend, even though he sued me personally for $100 million in 1985. The case was an antitrust suit, which awards triple damages, so $300 million was the full amount I might have owed Karsten if we — the USGA was defending me — had lost the case. There were other defendants as well, including my counterpart at the R&A and various other officials of both the USGA and the R&A.

The lawsuit dealt with the grooves in Ping's iron clubs. In 1984 I recommended a change to the groove specifications in the Rules of Golf, along with twenty or more other changes. It was a time when the rules were being reorganized, so it seemed a good time to clean up some aspects of the rules that had gotten a little shabby.

The existing rule stated that grooves had to be shaped like a V. Such grooves had traditionally been formed by rolling or stamping a groove into the face of a forged club. Thanks to Karsten's inspiration, this was no longer the main technique for putting grooves into clubfaces; investment casting could not produce a groove as well-defined as the rules required, and if we applied the rule as written then more than 60 percent of the clubs on the market would be nonconforming. The grooves that resulted from casting were "U" shaped, so we decided to change the rule to specify a depth and width rather than defining a groove by its width, flatness, and the angle of its side to the face plane. The new rule allowed grooves to be square-shaped, but with diverging sides and no sharp edges. Studies done as early as the 1960s indicated that under dry conditions the shape of the groove was irrelevant but the width and depth was important under grassy lie conditions — not heavy but light rough.

I knew Karsten was taking advantage of this, because he told me so in the locker room at Winged Foot during the 1984 U.S. Open. He made the grooves smaller than the maximum width, with a distance of three times the groove width between them; that ratio was the smallest separation the rules allowed. Unfortunately, because he'd also made the edges of the grooves relatively sharp, they cut the cover of the balls on every strike. Players who had to pay for their golf balls were upset at this added cost to their games, and the professionals didn't like seeing "feathers" on the ball after one impact. So Karsten decided to increase the size of the radius on the edge of the grooves — rounding them back and widening them at the opening — until they stopped doing such damage. This turned out to be a fairly significant radius, increasing the size of the groove. Without changing the groove pitch (the number of grooves per inch), the new ratio of groove-separation to groove-width was less than the required minimum of 3 to 1; it was about 2.3 to 1. I was made aware of this by a PGA official who questioned the conformity of Scott Verplank's Ping EYE2 irons based on an examination of the iron face using a jeweler's eyepiece with a special reticle attached. It was obvious that there was problem to everybody looking at it, and when the clubs were sent to the laboratory, sectioned, and examined under a microscope, they were found to be nonconforming.

Ping's argument was that the radius on the edge of the groove, even though it increased the size of the mouth of the groove, didn't increase the groove's width. The lawsuit pivoted on the question of how and where to make this measurement. We claimed it should be as the sketches so clearly demonstrated in the rule book —at the point where there was any substantial departure from the face plane. Karsten claimed the width of the groove should be measured at the bottom of the groove. This is equivalent to saying that the width of a canyon should be measured at the water level of the river that formed it. Maybe that's what Evel Knievel had in mind when he thought he could jump

his cycle over the Snake River Canyon; someone must have told him
the width measurement was made at the water level.

Karsten did make a very good point when he observed that the
difference between conforming and his nonconforming groove was
equivalent to the width of a human hair (about .003 of an inch).
This was true, but the entire groove itself was less than ten human
hairs wide. So if you want to be dramatic, you could say that the
$300 million suit was all about the width of a human hair. But that's
irrelevant. We'd ruled against balls that were too small by percentage
margins much smaller than this, or that were even .005 of an ounce
heavier than the maximum weight. These are inconsequential numbers
and meaningless when it comes to performance, but if there is to be
an objective precise specification, there has to be a line somewhere
(within manufacturing tolerances), and the degree of divergence isn't
the difference between conforming and nonconforming, the fact of
divergence beyond manufacturing tolerances is.

This little $300 million dispute is why Karsten and I didn't see
EYE2-eye for a while. It was ultimately settled without money
changing hands except from the USGA to its lawyers and Karsten
to his.

Once it was all over, Karsten surprised me with an unusual gesture.
Golf Digest had asked me and many prominent people in the game
to draw self-portraits in 1993, which would be auctioned publicly
to benefit our selected charities. My selection was MS (Multiple
Sclerosis).

Among all the portraits by the likes of Jack Nicklaus, Sam Snead,
Gary Player, Arnold Palmer, Tiger Woods, Greg Norman, Nick Price,
Davis Love III, Phil Mickelson, Charles Schulz of "Peanuts" fame,
and even Karsten Solheim, I didn't know how much my portrait

would be worth, but it immediately sold for $500 — and it was Karsten Solheim who bought it. I never found out what Karsten did with this original; I would not have been completely shocked to find it filled with dart holes or reprinted on rolls upon rolls of T-paper.

On second thought, I doubt he did either of these things, because I did consider him a friend; we just didn't agree on certain issues. I shed more than a few tears when I attended his posthumous — and belated — induction into the World Golf Hall of Fame.

Around the time that Karsten was introducing his first perimeter-weighted irons, I was working for Shakespeare Sporting Goods, having joined them after getting my engineering degree from Western Michigan University. Henry Shakespeare gave me a challenge: He wanted me to "design the best golf shaft the world has ever seen."

Shakespeare had introduced fiberglass shafts in the early 1960s, drawing on its experience with fishing rods. Gary Player was using the shafts, but the results weren't too satisfying. The material was heavy, similar in feel to a thick fishing rod. The problem was that all the fibers were running in the same direction, parallel to the axis of the shaft (good for fishing, but not good for golf, because the shaft has to resist some bending and twisting both — accommodate flexural and torsional stresses in technical language). When I got involved in 1968 I began experimenting with filament winding of the fibers: You weave bundles of fibers preimpregnated with epoxy resin back and forth in layers around a slowly turning steel mandrel (think of a lathe), and the cross-weave gives you the flexibility to design the flexural and torsional properties — stiffness and strength — you need.

Union Carbide found out that I was doing this research on golf shafts, working with new techniques of filament winding, and they asked if I would like to try to use graphite instead of glass. They were using graphite exclusively in the aerospace industry and wanted to introduce this material to the consumer market. They reasoned that a lot of corporate decision makers play golf, so if they could introduce the material into the game those executives would have to take notice of it and recognize its properties for other uses. This was a very clever idea, and today graphite is used in fishing rods, bicycles, masts for America's Cup yachts, spinnaker poles, propeller shafts, and nearly all of the structural work on some of the newest aircraft — I don't know if we can really take credit for all that, though the product wasn't going anywhere in a hurry until the consumer learned about it through golf and fishing and tennis applications.

Union Carbide sent me two to three pounds of graphite fibers — each fiber so small it takes fifty of them to reach the volume of a human hair — which cost about $500 a pound. (Fiberglass, by contrast, cost about $1.30 a pound, and steel about 30 cents a pound.) The material was very stiff, but not very strong for the stiffness, so it was unbalanced for use in a shaft. We worked with Union Carbide to balance the stiffness/strength properties of the fibers — less stiffness, more strength — and by surrounding each with a layer of epoxy resin and winding these bundles around a mandrel at specific selected angles, we were able to create a shaft that was half the weight of a steel shaft with the same flex and just as strong. An extra-stiff steel shaft weighed about four and a half ounces; with graphite, we could reduce that weight to just over two ounces without compromising performance.

This reduced weight was key; If you can reduce the overall weight of a club without taking any weight away from the head, you increase the head speed without any additional effort from the player. Increased speed without decreased head mass means increased ball speed and thus more distance. The quest for increased distance and reduced weight would shape the direction of equipment change over the next thirty years, and the graphite shaft — now virtually standard in woods — was an important first step.

We introduced the shaft at the PGA Merchandise Show in 1970, but we had a problem. We didn't have a patent on the shaft; the head of the division that included our R&D department at Shakespeare felt we shouldn't try to patent it, because in his view all a patent does is expose the details of your invention and the precise process to your competitors. Those competitors, he believed, can make minuscule alterations and go on to steal your idea and methods. He eventually retired and his successor decided this was not a good strategy and we needed protection on the product, but by then it was too late to file for a patent — too much time had elapsed since the product was first exposed to the public (to Jack Nicklaus, actually, by a member of our sales force).

Because we didn't have a patent, other companies quickly started making graphite shafts by a different process that resulted in an inferior product. The first Aldila version gave graphite a bad name; they couldn't control the torsional stiffness, and the shafts were like noodles. They used a flag-wrapping process rather than filament winding, which saved money but resulted in inconsistent properties; when you wrap sheets of fibers rather than wind individual bundles of fibers, you lose a lot of the control, resulting in inconsistent bending properties (a spine in the shaft), and to counter this the shaft has to be specifically oriented into the head to counter the effect of the spine. (A good shaft does not need to be specifically oriented in the head, even though many club fitters try to convince golfers otherwise and charge $20 or more to reorient even some good steel shafts.) It was several years before graphite shafts overcame that bad first impression. Today, this process has improved significantly and the quality has made a significant leap upward.

The shaft was readily accepted on Tour, but now only a few players use it in irons on the regular Tour. Seniors and women find it works well for them, and it's almost universally accepted in fairway woods and drivers and is making inroads in hybrids. It's a wonderful material, strong, light, and you can orient the separate bundles of fibers in the direction of the stresses that occur in the golf swing, which you can't do with a homogeneous material like steel. It's a literal space-age technology, brought to golf to make our swings a little more efficient.

Ironically, the graphite shaft has never been ruled on by the USGA. I submitted it and explained that because of its lighter weight, it might enable a golfer to hit the ball five or so yards farther than a comparable steel shaft. We never heard back from the USGA. I suppose I could have issued an approval ruling on it once I joined the USGA, but there was no reason to, as it had become an accepted part of the game.

Today, almost every golfer in the world has a graphite shaft somewhere in his or her bag, and I have no doubt that the concept is good and will eventually be accepted in irons on the regular Tour as it has been for seniors and ladies clubs. I believe that the use of graphite and the method devised to apply and process it to make a golf shaft has made a significant contribution to the game, making the game more enjoyable and implements more efficient. Not a bad innovation, now that I think about it.

The measure of a true innovation is acceptance. Marketers proclaim breakthroughs every day; each new club is the latest, greatest, purest, longest, finest, most advanced ever made. Tinkerers come up with new techniques and ideas just as often; most of the resulting products only make it out of the garage for a few attempts, thousands make it as far as the exhibition stalls at the PGA Show, but very few are still considered worthwhile a year or two later. The sign of a valuable innovation is that it gets imitated, and quickly.

As the 1970s and '80s progressed, this is exactly what happened with perimeter-weighted clubs. Karsten Solheim's breakthrough became an industry standard in fairly short order; manufacturers continued to make blades, but most recognized the demand for cavity-backed irons, and all came to see the benefits of casting over forging. Inevitably, some began to wonder about the possibility of applying this concept to make a more forgiving driver.

The trouble is, wood isn't metal. You can't start carving out holes in the back of a wooden head without compromising the integrity of the clubhead. Even hardwoods like persimmon or maple were prone to cracking if the hitting area was made too thin.

However, metal *is* metal. And in 1979, TaylorMade created a splash by introducing a driver with a head of stainless steel that its creator, Gary Adams, was certain would hit the ball farther than the wooden woods on the market.

Perhaps I should say "reintroducing," because the metalwood was not a new concept. The first patent for such a club was issued to William Currie, Jr. of Edinburgh in 1891. Currie's design consisted of a gunmetal casing filled with red gutta-percha that formed the club's face. Other 19th-century efforts involved metal shells that contained a wooden block in an effort to combine the strength of metal with the perceived feel and responsiveness of wood. Some echoed Currie's use of gutta-percha in replaceable faces for their metalwoods; breakage was a great concern in the age of handmade clubs with wooden shafts, and the chief advantage of metal was its relative imperviousness to routine damage. One enterprising designer put into his metal shell a wooden block backed with an elastic material, creating an early version of the springlike effect.

Golfers on all levels pretty much ignored these attempts at innovation and stayed with woods made of materials deserving of the name. Throughout the middle of the 20th century, it was still possible to find metal-headed drivers, but generally only at practice ranges, where they were available for use by swingers who'd neglected to bring their own clubs. An aluminum-headed club with a steel shaft was almost impossible to break, an important factor considering some of the ill-conceived swings on display at the average driving range.

But something changed in the 1970s, something that made the market ripe for the new form of metal-headed driver that Gary Adams developed and put on display for industry professionals. That something was the casting process of manufacture, which made it possible to create hollow metal clubheads. The central cavity could be filled with lightweight foam for stability, or even left empty to further reduce the weight of the head. TaylorMade metalwoods were not hard to make, did not require the labor-intensive finishing skills and care that wooden clubs required, and had a higher MOI than the wooden equivalent. These features were wonderful, but did not seem to be enough to supplant the traditional look, feel, and sound of a persimmon driver. I recall talking to Gary in the covered parking garages where all the manufacturers were exhibiting their equipment at one of the first West Coast PGA shows at Industry Hills, California. He was standing on his own, behind a bag with several metal-headed woods sticking out of it. Gary and I had quite a while to talk, because no one was expressing much interest in his clubs. He was a little down, but I think he really believed that this was something that would work and that golfers would buy them. One advantage of Gary's design is that the club had a built-in forgiveness factor. The weight was spread throughout the shell and actually improved on the forgiveness concept of cavity-back irons: When the center of your club is hollow, inevitably the weight is concentrated around the perimeter of the clubhead. Solheim had already demonstrated the value of this. To my knowledge and during my discussions with Gary, he didn't suggest that this was part of his thinking; he just thought his club would hit the ball farther.

Adams convinced PGA Tour pros Ron Streck and Jim Simons to give his new driver a try. In 1981, Streck became the first to win a PGA Tour event using a metalwood, at the rain-shortened Houston Open. Simons won the next year's Bing Crosby Pro-Am at Pebble Beach, and the widely televised event gave a boost of publicity to what had been derided on Tour as "a driving-range club." (Because Streck had come from far back in the field with a third-round 62, and because so few of his shots and none of his drives were shown on the telecast, even Gary Adams was unaware of Streck's distinction; for years after, he and most other commentators credited Simons with the first metal-aided victory.) In two years TaylorMade went from selling $47,000 worth of clubs to over $12 million. "Pittsburgh persimmon" was here to stay.

For the first several years of the metalwood generation, the clubs resembled traditional woods in every way but makeup. They were of similar volume, were connected to the shaft by a hosel, and had faces of similar dimension. They looked, in short, like science-fiction robotic versions of what was already familiar. Golfers could debate, if they wished, whether they were truly a substantial advance over the prevailing persimmon models. In fact, they were an incremental development, but not a revolutionary one.

Enter Ely Callaway. Unlike Karsten Solheim and Gary Adams, Callaway was no backyard tinkerer, nor did he have any engineering training. He was a businessman, one with faith in the marketability of a superior product, and he saw an opportunity in the golf club business, first acquiring the assets of Hickory Stick USA, a maker of replica hickory-shafted clubs for historical recreations and novelty purposes. As he had in his previous efforts in the textiles and wine-making businesses, Callaway surrounded himself with bright and innovative people, and encouraged them to think in nontraditional ways. Richard Helmstetter, in his role as Callaway's senior executive vice president directing club design, put together a team of aerospace and metallurgical engineers to ponder the next step in golf club evolution. Their first products, the S2H2 irons and woods (the name is a semi-acronym for "short, straight, hollow hosel"), hit the market in 1988 and 1989 respectively. They performed well, but not like the bombshell that came next.

In 1991, Callaway introduced the original Big Bertha. Named for the German long-range howitzer of World War I, it looked like no other golf club. It had no hosel; the shaft connected directly into the head. Its face resembled a smile, with the bottom edge rising to meet the top line at its corners. It was the biggest driver anyone had seen: a whopping 190 cc of stainless steel. Because of its size and its weight distribution, it had the biggest sweet spot and was more forgiving than any club that had ever been built. By the end of 1992, it was the number one driver on the Senior, Ladies, and Hogan (now Nationwide) Tours.

All of the advantages and more of Ping's irons were built into Callaway's drivers. And Big Bertha took one more essential step forward, recognizing the unique aspects of how a driver is used. Unlike every other club, a driver is designed to make contact with the ball on the upswing. Its target is not sitting down on the ground; it rests up in the air on a wooden pedestal. The profile of a Big Bertha wasn't necessarily useful for hitting a ball off a fairway lie, but it didn't have to be; its center of gravity was a little higher than wooden woods, it generally had more loft, and its final secret was that it was an inch longer than standard clubs. The combination of all of these properties made the Big Berthas the most successful woods in the history of the game. And it did on average hit the ball a little farther — not as much as was promoted or that golfers were claiming, but farther.

Persimmon holdouts might scoff at Bertha's size, comparing her and subsequent generations of drivers to swinging a vacuum cleaner by its hose, but Callaway's sales more than doubled with the introduction of its cannon, and its competitors were left with only one way to respond: imitate.

As Big Bertha grew in market share, it spawned dozens of big-headed brethren, all hovering around the 190 cc mark. The problem for club makers and metallurgists was that steel had its limits and drawbacks. As manufacturers tried to make larger clubheads with thinner steel walls to maintain the correct weight, they discovered that the clubfaces would collapse if they were made too thin. Kevlar, the fiber used in bulletproof vests, had a brief heyday, often combined with other plastics and even graphite, but it was merely an interim step.

Callaway Golf was determined to hold onto its now-challenged market share, and if it wanted to get even bigger, its clubheads would have to do the same. If Big was good, Bigger was better. But bigger would mean heavier, and heavier meant slower, so the gains from the even-further-enlarged sweet spot were offset by the losses to slower swing speeds. There were two and only two possibilities to explore if you wanted to feed the public's hunger for Newer and Bigger: make the walls of the club thinner and find a material lighter than steel but just as strong. Graphite wouldn't quite work, because it doesn't have the properties needed for the face of the club. (It is used today in the body of some clubheads for its light weight and structural strength.) Where could manufacturers turn?

Hello, titanium.

Atomic number 22, chemical symbol Ti, titanium in its pure form is a metal that is as strong as steel but 43 percent lighter. In the compound form titanium dioxide (TiO_2), the element has long been an essential part of golf: its most frequent commercial use is in white pigment, it's what makes a lot of white things white, whether it's in toothpaste or in the paint that covers a golf ball. (Almost every golf ball has titanium in it, or at least on it — a fact that those who tried to market balls on the basis of titanium flecks in the core probably didn't want you to know.)

Its lightness and strength make titanium a vital part of modern airplane technology, particularly in the engines. It is extremely resistant to corrosion, even when immersed long-term in sea water, and is used in the manufacture of ship propeller shafts and rigging, and increasingly in pipelines for offshore drilling. It tends not to react with biomass in general, which makes it an excellent choice for bone implants, especially since it can be safely exposed to magnetic resonance imaging tests, unlike many other metals.

Titanium offered all the attributes a club maker could ask for, and when Callaway introduced the first titanium-headed driver, the Great Big Bertha in 1995, it weighed less than its predecessor despite being 30 percent larger at 250 cc. Not only was this larger head more forgiving — the farther away from the center of gravity you move the weight in the shell (walls) of the clubhead, the bigger the effective sweet spot will be — but it seemed to hit the ball even longer than anything that came before.

Titanium seemed too good to be true, the Magic Bullet of golf-club design. Freed from the constraints of steel, high-tech designers could use computer modeling to devise ever-bigger and ever-better drivers. In four years, Bertha had grown from a Big 190 cc to a Great 250 cc. It took just two years for Callaway to try to protect its stance in the industry by rolling out its Biggest model at 290 cc. Golfers seemed willing to spend $500 for the giant new club that helped them hit the ball farther and straighter. The size race was on, and competitors were firing from all sides.

In the middle of all of this, I got a phone call in my role as Technical Director of the USGA, from the R&D department of TaylorMade reporting that it had been running some tests on Callaway's club, and their chief researcher had come up with some unusual results from clubs with thin titanium faces, results that were too consistent to be anomalies. The ball was coming off the face of these clubs at speeds greater than the testers and analysts expected. The only possible explanation was that the faces had a springlike effect, actually propelling the ball forward while it was in contact with the club. It was suggested that we take a look at this, as it was against the rules as they understood them.

I'll discuss at length in chapter six the series of events that followed from this call. For now, I'll just say that they were right in what they observed, i.e., that the titanium faces were actually deforming and reforming while still in contact with the ball, enhancing its velocity, and this was in conflict with the rules that prohibited a club from having the effect of a spring. Despite this, it was decided by the Executive Committee that we — the USGA, with the R&A following suit — would accept a certain amount of spring-like effect in these drivers, so long as their coefficient of restitution (COR) was no greater than 0.83. (I'll explain coefficient of restitution in the next chapter.)

The manufacturers weren't doing this intentionally; they were trying to make their clubs more forgiving by moving more and more weight away from the face to the perimeter. Because titanium was so strong, they could make the faces thinner and thinner without having them collapse at impact; they finally stretched it so thin that it actually functioned like a trampoline. This was an unintended byproduct with revolutionary implications.

Golfers have been swinging clubs for five hundred years. In all that time — half a millennium! — the power behind a golf shot came from the speed generated by the golfer's swing, the mass represented by the clubhead, and the resiliency of the ball as it flattens against the clubface and rebounds forward towards the target (we hope). Now, for the first time, the clubface was making the impact more efficient and adding speed to the ball, shooting it forward with an extra little oomph.

This was initially only true for drivers with a big, thin titanium face that provided the trampoline effect, but as soon as the COR limit was established, how could you limit it to drivers? If increased COR was good for drivers, it must also be good for other clubs, right? As expected, manufacturers have tried to market their fairway woods with high COR — but it doesn't have the same appeal as it does for the "Big Stick." The major advantage for other clubs in using titanium is that it gives the designer a little more flexibility to move the weight around and increase the MOI, which helps with forgiveness but doesn't add significant distance.

But with drivers, yes, there is a distinct difference in distance. This is true even if you don't swing as fast as a professional. At a swing speed of 95 mph, a legal-limit titanium clubhead will give you an extra fifteen yards when you hit it on the sweet spot, but we don't do this often enough to make quite that big a difference in the length of our average drive. For us, the gains may not be as large as we think they are, but they're still not so small that you should throw them back.

The story of the titanium driver is an object lesson in how many incremental steps it takes until a truly significant breakthrough took place. TaylorMade revives the metalwood and uses the casting process to make it more forgiving; any gain in length was mostly an illusion except that off-center hits didn't lose as much as with persimmon. Callaway makes the club bigger, which makes it slightly more forgiving, but probably not so much so that the average golfer can tell the difference. Then many manufacturers join in and come out with their own super-duper advances, each of which proclaims itself to be revolutionary but in fact is only repeating the efforts of others. Those copycats force Callaway to think bigger, which means lighter materials are required, which leads to trying titanium, which lets everyone make the clubs even bigger and the faces thinner —

which finally makes a real difference, although not until it breaks the rules to get there.

In forty years of constant tinkering and countless declarations of a new and improved era, there are three and only three innovations that mean anything significant to your game (and one of them came about by accident!): perimeter weighting, first in irons and then in metal woods; the graphite shaft that everybody uses now, and titanium drivers with thin enough faces to create a springlike effect. If you have these in your bag, you don't need anything else. In real terms, nothing else will make a lot of difference.

CHAPTER FOUR: Time Out for Science

The comedian Tommy Smothers once proposed a book entitled *Thirty-Six Things to Think About During Your Backswing*. The subject of this chapter is the science involved in hitting a golf ball — don't worry, it's not a schoolbook lesson, but an understandable explanation of what happens during that brief interval we call contact. I can tell you right up front that you'd be wise to forget about all of it while you're standing over your next shot. Thoughts of spin rates, gear effects, and moment of inertia won't help you get the club on plane or square it at impact, but they will help you talk about and select equipment that's right for you. You don't really need to know any of this to play the game, but without it we're all just walking.

The game of golf is basically very simple: You tee up the ball, aim, and hit it. I'll assume you can tee up the ball just fine; for about eighty years that has meant sticking a peg in the ground, but the game was played quite nicely when it involved building little mounds of wet sand instead. (Laura Davies doesn't use a tee, but has been very successful in hitting the ball a long way after pounding the ground with her club to create a raised surface.) Aiming is a matter for your local pro to address; nobody's ever written a book on the subject that I know of, though the game would be played much better if someone did. But hitting it — ah, there's an activity that can fill up volumes.

The golf swing is a complicated method of performing a simple task: transferring momentum from you through the shaft to the clubhead, which must then collide with an object at rest (the ball). In this violent collision between head and ball, which only lasts one-half of a millisecond, something's got to give. It used to be only the ball, but we've now designed clubs that can be said to both "give" and "forgive." These two phenomena have significantly changed the performance properties of the game's equipment in recent years, as we saw in chapter three.

Let's talk about the "giving" thing first. At impact, there is a violent collision in which an average of about 1,700 pounds of force is exchanged over the period of .00045 seconds in which the club and ball are in contact. This is an extremely short period of time — almost unthinkably short. Almost.

It takes about 0.1 seconds to blink your eye or to wink. In the duration of that blink, 222 impacts of driver and ball could take place if you were using an old persimmon driver. With a new-fangled titanium driver, there would be time for 208 such collisions, because the ball stays on the face of the titanium driver for slightly longer than that of persimmon or other materials that have been used for the purpose.

You've seen super-slow motion video or film of the ball at impact, and you've no doubt noticed how dramatically it flattens before springing back and taking off to parts known or unknown. The technical term for this is deformation and recovery. The ball deforms at impact as it acquires compressed springlike energy, then travels along with the club while it recovers its shape in the process of expending some of that energy, pushing off the clubhead, and taking flight.

What you may not have noticed in watching the slow-mo is that the face of the club also deforms at impact. All driver faces give at impact

— persimmon, steel, titanium, porcelain, moon rock, whatever you want to try. The unique quality of a thin-faced titanium driver is that it will deform considerably more than other clubfaces, and because of its properties will not collapse or yield but actually recovers during the unimaginably brief duration of impact. This is the "giving" aspect of titanium that gives extra yardage to our drives.

Things happen so fast while the club and ball are in contact that we can barely appreciate it, never mind exert any control over the process. I am sometimes asked about the value of the feedback we get from how we "feel" the club and ball at impact and if there is anything we can do at that time to correct a shot we know will be imperfect.

Those who ask the question don't understand how short a time impact lasts, versus how long it takes for messages about it to reach our brains. Studies show that by the time we are able to react to anything that happens at impact, the ball is nearly 20 yards down range. In other words, once you've initiated contact with the ball, you may as well try to control the ball by talking to it as by any physical means. Moreover, even if we could do something in time, it would not have any effect, because the part of the club that's in our hands — the shaft — plays no role in the collision nor affects the transfer of energy once impact has begun. Once clubface meets ball, our only relevant task is to hang onto the club to make sure it doesn't go flying down the fairway.

The fact that the clubface now adds momentum to the transaction between club and ball means that the ball can be propelled at a velocity never before seen from similar swing speeds. Engineers would say that the momentum transfer has become more efficient; golfers describe the same phenomenon with the phrase "20 extra yards," or perhaps "you da man!" There is a precise measure of the efficiency of transfer; it is called the coefficient of restitution, abbreviated COR to the cognoscenti, of whom you are now one. Drop COR into your next conversation about equipment and you'll sound very smart. Keep reading and you'll know what it means.

Coefficient of restitution is determined by dividing the separation velocity of the two colliding bodies by the approach velocity before the collision. To take a simple example, let's assume that a ball is flung at a solid brick wall (nongiving and with infinite mass) at 100 mph, and it rebounds from the wall at 75 mph. This gives us a COR of 0.75 for that collision. This is essentially the COR of the ball, because the wall is assumed not to be contributing anything other than its hardness and its mass.

If a ball could rebound at the same speed at which it approached the wall, the collision would be considered perfectly elastic with no energy lost in the collision: a COR of 1.0. This would be perfectly efficient. It is also considered impossible. Among other things, you would have to imagine that such a collision was completely silent, because the bang you hear means that some energy has been converted into sound. There are also internal losses involved in the flattening, twisting, and recovery of the ball as well as some complex frictional forces.

When driver heads were made of persimmon, their contribution to the speed of the ball was based entirely on the speed, hardness, and weight (mass) of the swinging clubhead. From a "giving" point of view, older clubs — including the early hollow metal drivers — were very passive during impact. Yes, they gave (deformed) a little, but any recovery that took place did nothing to enhance ball speed. This, however, is no longer the case; driver heads have become active participants.

As I described in the last chapter, this property of titanium clubheads was developed inadvertently, but has become an essential feature of their value to golfers. Let's walk through the calculations and see how much we've gained.

Take a collision in which the clubhead is moving at 110 mph before impact and is slowed to 76 mph by the collision with the ball (a realistic estimate), and the ball is launched at a speed of 160 mph. The COR consists of the separation velocity (ball speed minus the head speed after impact) divided by the approach velocity (head speed before impact): 160 minus 76 is 84, divided by 110 gives us a COR of .764, which is roughly the COR of the collision between a persimmon driver and a fairly good ball. (Obviously, the resilience of the ball is a factor, but we'll hold that constant for a moment.)

When we introduce a titanium head, the equation takes the same form, but now the resilience of the face joins the resilience of the ball in affecting the energy transfer. The ball stays in contact with the club for longer, and the head slows down a little more. The numbers would still show an approach velocity of 110 mph, but now the post-impact velocity of the head is reduced to 74 mph, while the ball is launched at a speed of 165 mph. Separation velocity is now 91 mph (165 minus 74), divided by 110 mph, gives us a COR of .827. This springlike effect has increased ball speed by 5 mph, which will translate on its own to a little less than 10 extra yards both in carry and overall distance on standard turf. Factor in a change in launch conditions (to be discussed later), and you gain another 5 to 10 yards, depending on where you started from. Add in a ball with greater resilience — the move from wound balls to solid three-piece balls came after the introduction of titanium — and you tack on another 5 yards or so. This accounts for the 25-yard increase in driving distance on Tour between 1995 and 2006.

When the USGA set the limit for COR at .83, it did so out of fear that some super new material would come along that would be an even more profound advance over titanium than titanium had been over persimmon, and that people will be hitting 400-yard drives before long without radically increasing their head speed. (If that was its fear, then why didn't it simply enforce the existing rule that still states, "The material and construction of, or any treatment to, the face or clubhead must not have the effect at impact of a spring..."? We had already changed from language written in 1909 that referred to "a contrivance such as a spring," recognizing the possibility that something like titanium might arrive that would have the same effect without being extrinsic to the club itself. I could go on for days about this, and sometimes have.) That fear was unnecessary.

We all know that a ball will never bounce back higher than from where it was dropped. If you think for one moment that such a thing is possible, ask yourself the following: What happens on the next bounce, and the next? We could free ourselves from dependence on imported oil just by using the energy being created by these bouncing balls. Alas, no such balls exist, nor can they.

Consider, however, a ball dropped not onto a hard surface, but onto a hard surface with a trampoline fixed atop it. This is the springlike effect we have been talking about. Now we have a combination of the resilience of the ball and the efficient energy stored in, and released from, the trampoline — but we still will never achieve a perfect transfer of energy, never get that ball to bounce higher than the point from which it started. We have improved the transfer, but we can never perfect it.

There are limits to the probable COR for this transaction. The practical limit is a little above .93 or so. So even if there were no limit placed in the rules of golf on the COR for any club, most likely the maximum to be gained from improving this particular aspect of equipment would be another 8 to 10 yards — less than what we can gain by exercising and becoming more flexible. Even without the questionably adopted regulation — defending chastity by saying it's okay to be a little bit pregnant — golfers and designers were going to have to look elsewhere for the magic extra 20 yards that is claimed (implicitly or explicitly) by every new innovation.

Let's now consider the "forgiving" part of a club's design, an aspect that has altered but not changed the game.

Most of us, if we are to get on with our lives and not waste our personal energy in petty grudges, learn to ignore or overlook the human errors that haunt us in nearly every walk of life. We truly wish that others — waiters who bring us the wrong food; cabbies who barrel through a red light when we're trying to cross the street; checkout clerks who miss or double-scan an item at the grocery store — would get better at what they do, or at least be better at it when they intersect with us. But since that's not likely to happen, and anyway we have no control over them, we have to become more forgiving.

From the point of view of our golf clubs and balls, we are those waiters, motorists, and clerks. They wish we would get better, but since we don't, they need to allow for our errors, to have more forgiveness built into them.

Is it really so hard, they ask us, to learn to hit the ball on the sweet spot and towards the target? The ball doesn't much like rattling around the tree trunks, and the club doesn't appreciate the way it gets jerked around during the collision, or then is whacked against the ground in punishment when the error is ours. All we have to do is to hit the ball on the carefully engineered sweet spot of the club with the face pointing and going in the right direction. Admittedly, this is not so simple a task when the face is at the end of a stick some 44 inches long, traveling at close to 100 mph or more. But it can be learned, if we would only practice it every day for hours on end.

This we will not do. "I haven't got the time," we tell ourselves. "I'm not coordinated enough." "I can't concentrate that long." There are many reasons why we don't master this act, just as our waiters and clerks have reasons for what we see as their incompetence.

So rather than develop mastery, we get the most forgiving implements available, because this is our leisure, and the truth is, we want to get out there and start doing rather than spending hours upon hours preparing. If we're going skiing, and we want to get out there as quickly as possible, we get the biggest, fattest, most parabolic skis on the market. These certainly aren't the kind of skis that will win an Olympic medal for anybody, but they'll do a good job of getting us down the slope without killing ourselves and will let us have fun doing it. After all, we're out to have a good time, not necessarily to be the fastest skier we can be.

In golf, however, we have a bit of a dilemma, because we really do want to be better than we are, and just getting around the course with our limbs intact isn't good enough. Yet we'd rather not have to do all that hard work, especially not if we can simply buy our way to our dreams. Manufacturers know all about this frailty of ours, and they cater to it. They know that they can't really build a Magic Club that will bring our dreams to life, but they know how to imply otherwise and to sell us what we desire, which is hope. Designers can't create magic, but they can provide forgiveness, so that when we miss the sweet spot the effect of the error will be minimized.

The technical term that governs a club's forgiveness is its moment of inertia (MOI) — another acronym you can use when you want to sound like you know important things about equipment. MOI is the measure of resistance to angular acceleration — in golf terms, the resistance to twisting during imperfect impact with the ball (not on the sweet spot), twisting that significantly affects the ball's trajectory, distance, or direction relative to its intended target. We're very target-oriented in golf, but to explain MOI in more concrete terms I'm going to focus solely on the phrase "resistance to twisting."

Here's an experiment for you that will demonstrate differences in MOI. Take two golf clubs and hold them together with their shafts overlapping by 12 inches and their grips on the outside ends. With your hands clamping the clubs in place, rotate them in front of you like a propeller, first clockwise and then changing to counterclockwise fairly quickly. You'll experience some resistance every time you change direction. Now reconfigure the clubs so that the overlap is the same, but the grips are in the middle and the heads are on the outside. Go through the same rotations as before at the same speed. You'll notice a significantly larger resistance to changing direction than you felt before.

The overall weight of the assembly has not changed, just the configuration. What you have done is to move more of the weight (the clubheads) away from the center of rotation. You have increased the MOI of the system by moving the weight as far away as possible from the center of gravity (the balance point around which you were rotating the clubs).

That's what MOI is. And this is exactly what Karsten Solheim was doing with his first toe-heel weighted putters and his perimeter-weighted irons and what every manufacturer of a hollow metal-headed driver is doing today in his laboratory. Moving weight outward, away from the center of gravity (which is generally behind the center of the clubface), increases the MOI, which is the fancy way of saying it makes them more forgiving.

Actually, club makers have become even fancier, because they're distributing weight not merely towards the toe and heel of the club but also up and down and backward. In the two-club twisting example above, that would mean taking some of the weight that was distributed at the ends of the assembly and putting an additional shaft at a right angle to the first two with some of its weight concentrated at the top and bottom. The MOI has been increased in two directions, giving us an even greater margin for error. More trespasses forgiven, on misses not only toward the toe and heel but also up and down on the face.

Because elite players may be tempted, thanks to the forgiveness factor, to make a more violent swing at the ball and drive it farther, the USGA has introduced a limit on MOI about the vertical axis (toe-heel forgiveness). I think this is terribly wrong-headed. I share the concern others express about the "giving" quality of titanium clubs, though I wouldn't waste time quibbling about fractions of levels of COR; all springlike effect should have been kept out of the game if the USGA were serious about regulating the distance the pros can hit the ball, but since it wasn't, the degree of openness of the barn door is irrelevant to me and to the long-gone horse. When it comes to forgiveness, however, I'm in favor of as much as manufacturers can build into a modern club. You see, a generous COR is of greatest value to the best players, those who hit the ball most often on the sweet spot. But high-MOI clubs do the most good for the less skilled, we poor wretches who seek all the indulgence for our sins we can find.

The pros and the scratch amateurs make such consistent contact on the sweet spot — they have put in the hours of work to perfect this — that, beyond a very limited range, they don't need added forgiveness. If they do miss the sweet spot by a significant amount, they will lose distance, which is penalty enough in their competitions. When it comes to regulating equipment, I favor as much help for the average golfer as possible, especially if it matters as little to the game's elite as the placement of the white and red tees, or whether a water hazard is 100 or even 200 yards away from the tee.

Before we move on to further consideration of distance and its limits, let's take a spinning class.

An amateur once asked Tommy Armour how he could get more backspin on his shots like the impressive ones hit by famous professionals. "Do your approach shots go past the hole, or are they usually someplace short?" Armour asked. When his student admitted that he usually hits the ball short, the Silver Scot thundered, "Then what the hell do you want backspin for????"

A good question. Nonetheless, everyone who picks up a club wants to emulate those dazzling displays where the ball goes flying onto the green, takes two bounces, and then magically backs up to behind where it landed. Here's a piece of nice news for you: Your shots already have backspin — not enough to make them do yo-yo tricks, but some.

It would be very difficult to hit a shot that didn't have backspin. The club would have to have no loft at all, approach the ball on a straight horizontal and level path, and strike a ball teed exactly at the height of the center of gravity of the clubhead. Anything else and you're generating backspin, even with the putter. This is a good thing, since the spin — in conjunction with the ball's dimples, which create a rough surface — modifies the airflow over the ball and creates the lift forces that allow the ball to fly as far as it does. A ball without spin will fly only about 140 yards, compared to a ball with spin that goes 260 yards if all else is equal.

The amount of spin varies significantly, depending mainly on the loft of the club. A driver with a loft of 10 degrees will spin the ball at about 2,500 to 3,000 revolutions per minute, while a wedge with a loft of 55 degrees spins it at 8,000 to 10,000 rpm or more. Other factors that influence the amount of spin are:

(1) the approach angle of the club (a downward blow changes the effective loft angle of the club face, producing more spin);

(2) the location of the impact point on the clubface and its relation to the center of gravity of the clubhead;

(3) the construction of the ball (generally speaking, a softer cover will create more spin than a harder cover — in today's solid balls, two layers of covers enable the ball to spin more off the wedges and less off the driver);

(4) the playing conditions, such as fairway or rough. In almost all cases, a ball will get less spin out of light rough than from the fairway, because moisture in the form of grass comes between the ball and the clubface; the exceptions come with a 5-iron or less lofted club, which actually gets a little more spin out of light rough than from the fairway;

(5) the surface roughness of the clubface in the form of grooves and/ or sandblasting (experiments show that under dry conditions the maximum spin rate comes when the face is sandblasted without grooves, but from light rough or grassy conditions the grooves are essential to obtain the desired spin); and finally

(6) the speed of the clubhead (the faster the speed, the more spin, though this is not as much of a factor as loft or surface roughness).

During the brief moments of contact between ball and clubface, a lot happens. When a lofted club makes contact, the ball first slides, then as it deforms (flattens out) it sticks to the face and starts rolling up the face, its rotational speed increasing quickly. Three processes are taking place simultaneously: The ball is flattening against the advancing clubface, it is sliding up the face, and it is beginning to spin. Friction between the clubface and the ball, present because of the surface roughness and the grooves, bring the sliding to a halt and increase the rate at which the ball is spinning.

For driving clubs with low lofts, the friction is enough (even without grooves) to stop the sliding motion and convert it to a rolling motion up the clubface. Soon after the ball starts its recovery process, both from the flattening and the winding up, the spin rate of the ball is as great as it can be for any given shot. The cover of the ball is no longer moving relative to the clubface and is sticking to the face because of the frictional forces. It is at this stage of impact that the ball is starting to bounce off the face and unwind. At the very last moment before the ball leaves the face, the frictional forces are reduced and the ball slides a little more. Then, finally, the ball is propelled onward by the process of recovery along with the forward momentum imparted to it.

If blades of grass come between the face and the ball, it will slide for longer on the face and will release a little earlier. If there is enough grass — 4 inches of good, juicy, thick stuff — it may never completely stick to the face. Since maximum spin is generated when the ball is starting to unwind while still stuck to the face, if it never sticks it will never get maximum spin, so the ball will leave the face at a higher speed with a higher launch angle than expected (because energy was not used to generate spin). We call this "a flyer."

This concise explanation of spin should address the practical question of how to put more spin on your shots with a three-fold answer: (1) Increase the effective loft by hitting down on the ball, which is tough because if you don't hit it on the money you may have a lot of dirt between the club and the ball. This really fat shot kills distance, eliminates spin, and embarrasses you in front of your friends. (2) Try to keep the ball out of the rough. (3) Swing harder: the faster the impact speed, the more ball speed and backspin.

Distance is the great double-edged sword of golf. The long hitter is celebrated and envied, but at the same time he raises outcries that the game of finesse and precision is being destroyed by the deployment of his prolific talents. Equipment makers cater to those who seek that elusive 20 extra yards, declaring that their wares will make your shots farther, higher, faster. And rules makers try to ensure that those claims are at least somewhat apocryphal, so that improvement stems from the ability of the player rather than the make of equipment.

Distance is both a goal and a problem. Everyone wants to hit the ball farther, but if everyone hits the ball farther, then either the game becomes easier or the course has to be lengthened constantly. So manufacturers and ruling bodies are in a perpetual dance of offense and defense, gambit and counter, like chess players operating in steel and plastics.

The birth of the ruling bodies in the 1890s coincided with the first great panic over distance, the first declaration that new technology was making the classic courses obsolete. At every stage, the standards are set on the basis of what the standard makers are able to measure.

The increase in distance that we've observed over the years is not entirely due to the ball. Other factors, such as improved physical skills and physiological and psychological conditioning, as well as improved course conditions, have contributed significantly and are probably the major determinants — but we can't control those things, and so we focus on the ball.

When the Haskell ball was introduced in 1898, it was livelier than its predecessors, and while it helped popularize the game, it alarmed the powers that were. Measuring what they could, in 1920 they set limits on the size and weight of a golf ball, believing this would standardize and restrict the performance of the ball. It did not, and so in 1942 a resilience standard was approved that was supposed to totally control distance. This Initial Velocity Standard declared that a ball could not exceed a velocity of 250 feet per second when struck by a calibrated impact machine, with a test tolerance of 2 percent to cover variances in equipment and test procedures.

This idea was fine as far as it went, using the technology of the day to measure what it could, but it didn't take into account the way the aerodynamics of a ball could change, mostly through improved dimple configurations. In 1974, I took on the task of developing an Overall Distance Standard for the USGA as its Technical Director, trying to consider — without isolating — all the factors that affect how far a ball could travel. With an ODS in place, we reasoned, it wouldn't matter if someone tried to develop a more resilient ball or a new kind of cover or a set of dimples in various shapes, sizes, numbers, or patterns — if it went too far under the uniform measuring conditions, it was non-conforming.

The standard, compared to how we determine these things today, was relatively crude. It relied on a mechanical golfer — the legendary Iron Byron — that closely replicated the swing of a real golfer in order to strike balls in a manner similar to a long-hitting professional. A specific clubhead speed was chosen using a "standard" head weight and construction. The distance a ball traveled after it landed on a manicured fairway at our outdoor test range was measured and compared to our arbitrarily chosen standard of 280 yards. We selected 280 yards on the basis of the performance of the longest ball available at the time we developed the standard in 1975.

ODS worked fairly well for its time. It was, however, a nightmare to manage. We were constantly coping with variations stemming from the outdoor conditions wind, temperature, firmness of the turf — that resulted in unacceptably wide tolerances and results that were hard for manufacturers to duplicate in their own testing.

If every golfer hit the ball the same way, at the same speed and with the same club, the test procedure would have been acceptable, and it was the best we could do with the technology of the time. In the late 1970s, though, we were on the cusp of a revolution in information-processing; the computer was about to change everything in both design and testing.

We know now, more clearly than we did thirty years ago, that differences in golf ball construction are reflected in how they leave the clubface. Spin rates, speeds, and launch angles vary from one make of ball to another even when the club contacts both the same way every time. Every ball hit by Iron Byron has its own trajectory height, flight time, and bounce-and-roll distance; in some cases, these conditions might be ideal for that particular ball, but in other cases it might not. The mechanical golfer reflected the understanding we had of the kinematics of the swing when it was built and designed, but we have learned a great deal since then; computer trajectory simulations have shown that the ideal launch angle, for example, is higher than we had thought. If a ball's optimal launch conditions matched those of the test, the standard would function properly; however, if a ball happened to underperform at those conditions, we would wind up approving a ball that goes too far when it's launched at its own optimal conditions in the field. It's the equivalent of judging some speeding cars on a flat stretch, but others on a steep upgrade.

Computer modeling became the vehicle for improved testing. We started in the late 1980s to develop a method of measuring the aerodynamic properties of a golf ball This would allow us to simulate the distance a ball could travel more accurately than the actual test outdoors, because we could control the temperature, wind speed, atmospheric pressure, and even turf roll conditions.

The aerodynamic test went beyond the traditional method of passing air over a spinning ball in a confined chamber (wind tunnel), launching the ball with controlled spin and speed through a calm body of air. Measurements were made as the ball passed each of a series of stations on its way down a 70-foot range. We used combinations of different speeds and spin rates similar to what a ball would experience in flight. Plugging this information into the simulation program enabled us to calculate its complete trajectory and flight time, and a second model derived its bounce and roll under standardized conditions. The simulations allowed us to vary the launch angle and spin rate, to maximize the distance (optimize) for every ball and speed.

The overall test procedure is called Optimization, because it lets us determine the maximum distance each ball will travel under its own optimal launch conditions. Reflecting the improved equipment and better understanding of ideal contact, we would need to set the maximum distance in 1999 at about 305 yards, a substantial increase over the previous 280-yard mark (which was actually 296.8 when the test tolerance was taken into account).

In 1999, I proposed we adopt this "Mother of all tests" that would never again need to be adjusted and would indirectly cope with any advances in ball technology that might affect distance.

I called the procedure Optimized Overall Distance Standard, because it would let us determine the maximum distance each ball would travel under its own optimal launch conditions. If a manufacturer decided to change the aerodynamic or any other properties, it would not matter; the optimum launch conditions would be determined, and each ball would be tested at those specifications. There would be no need to adjust the test's fixed spin rate and launch angle whenever the test seems to be outdated, as is now the case.

Even if every ball tested under the new, more efficient test procedure were conforming, there would have to be a new limit established at about 305 yards (up from the present 280). The balls themselves would be unchanged, but the increase would come from testing them at their own ideal launch conditions. This kind of tailoring is extremely cumbersome with a mechanical golfer, but is easily achieved through simulation using the computer.

The beauty of Optimization, as opposed to Initial Velocity or the Overall Distance Standard, is its flexibility; test conditions move with ball design. There are no standard settings, other than a standard head impact speed equivalent to the longest hitters on Tour. It would provide a language in which to conduct the discussion about distance, a discussion that has grown more heated as the years have passed.

Unfortunately, the proposed Optimized ODS was rejected. I'd say there were three reasons for this.

First, I don't think the committee understood it or how it worked or how it would eliminate the need for constant future adjustments.

Second, a few companies complained that the average launch conditions for the pros were less than "optimum," and therefore the test didn't represent how golfers were really hitting the ball. I tried to explain that this ODS was not a golfer standard but a ball standard. It didn't matter what the golfers were actually doing, we were setting a limit, and the limit would be a realistic calibrated standard that would remain constant far into the future.

Third, the announced limit in yards would have to increase substantially from 280 in order to keep us from disapproving many balls that had been previously accepted. The committee believed that this would imply an increase to the standard, when what they really wanted to do was roll it back. In fact, it would merely recognize that the mechanical golfer no longer reflected the swing speed of the modern professional.

So the proposed Optimized ODS was rejected, largely for PR reasons. The USGA could not envision explaining to those who are paranoid about distance how its new and improved testing procedures would "increase the distance limit by about 25 yards." Of course, it would do no such thing, but the administrators didn't think they could tell the real story well enough, or maybe they simply didn't understand it themselves.

In the years since, the USGA has announced a change to the ODS. It reflects a higher swing speed, increasing the permitted distance under test procedures to 320 yards. The Executive Committee understands this, because they believe that the pros of today swing far faster than pros of thirty years ago.

The Overall Distance Standard will eventually move towards optimization, because it's the only sensible way to measure such a wide variety of ball types and configurations. The USGA is inching in that direction with its proposal to change the test conditions as appropriate. Once they start tinkering, it's only a matter of time before Optimization takes hold.

So things are not all bad, it's just going to take a little more time to get to the goal line. The game is about five hundred years old, so we can wait another five or ten for the USGA to get things right.

CHAPTER FIVE: Equipment Essentials

We take a lot for granted in the game of golf. Just because we've been immersed in the game and surrounded by equipment, we assume that we know what to look for when deciding how to find the right tools for our needs. Even worse, we equate price with quality and fanciness with appropriateness and assume that what's newest and latest is always what's best.

Golf equipment makers are in the business of selling things. If they can get you to think that this year's $500 driver is a significant improvement over last year's $500 driver, they've done their job. But just as the word "NEW!" on your toothpaste tube doesn't mean that your previous brand will make your teeth decay, the presence of a new model club or ball doesn't mean that the stuff you already own is holding you back. Chances are it's doing just fine.

The market for golf equipment is not growing and the competition is fierce, so product lines are in a constant fight for space in the stores. Declaring something to be New! Improved! and backing it with advertising dollars makes your local or national retailer pay attention and award the product some precious space on the show floor. Some things get changed for change's sake, or to improve aesthetics, and may actually worsen your performance. As we saw in chapters two and three, real innovations happen at broad intervals, not in constant rotation. The basic laws of physics and the design principles that utilize them don't change very much from year to year.

Having said that, I also know that the golf club or ball you have confidence in is the one that works best. This is why new clubs always seem to do so well for us: We feel good when we take them out of our bags, they're shiny and new, they don't know our faults yet, and they've never dumped a shot into the lake guarding the green. We expect to hit the ball well with new clubs, and those expectations have a powerful psychological effect. In medicine, it's called the placebo effect — the observed phenomenon that a pill or shot or treatment with no organic value to you may cause your symptoms to go away and even reverse an ailment's course. It doesn't mean you were faking; your belief in the treatment can lead your body to respond. So it is with a new hybrid, a driver, a sand wedge: Our confidence is expressed in a confident, affirmative swing, and a good shot follows.

I don't want to take away or lessen that wonderful effect. I want you to be able to view all your equipment, old or new, with the confidence that comes from knowing they are as advanced and as effective as you need them to be to play your best. You'll attack the course with a newfound sense that you haven't left any extra distance, fairways hit, or putts holed in the store where you either chose one club over another, or where you decided that you didn't need that Biggest Big Better club after all.

FIRST THINGS FIRST

The most expensive club in the bag, the biggest investment for most golfers, is the driver. From a standpoint of pure raw materials, that might make a little sense: It has the longest shaft and the largest head, and presumably these components enter into a decision on pricing. A little. Maybe.

Nah.

The driver costs the most because it's the Big Stick, the sexy swaggering leader of the pack, the Alpha Dog, the weapon we choose when we're taking the full measure of ourselves and our fellow golfers — when we're seeing Who's Longest (nudge-nudge wink-wink). We use it at the point on the course where everybody stands together, and where we can most enjoy the oohs and aahs of the rest of our foursome. (Be honest: Are you more satisfied when you hit a long drive or when you make a long putt? Are you sure?)

Put aside the ego implications and the driver's importance shrinks somewhat. We use it, on average, at most fourteen times a round, and probably should use it less often than that. We don't generally give as much thought to our putters, which we use more like thirty-plus times a round, or our wedges, which we know are called the scoring clubs — and isn't the point of the game to score as low as possible? But, no, we want to be as long as we can even more than we want our scores as low as they can get. Don't believe me? Ask yourself how much of your practice time is spent hitting drivers, how often you've switched drivers in the last ten years, and when was the last time you took a putting lesson. Or ask yourself how many ads you've seen for drivers, as opposed to irons or wedges or putters. Or when you last saw a ball claim to be the straightest on the market.

In chapters three and four we discussed the developments in driver technology over the last ten-to-fifteen years, how they came to be and how and why they work. If you haven't purchased a new driver in the last five years, you really ought to, in order to take advantage of the rewards of today's technology.

For a clubhead speed of about 110 miles per hour — around average on the PGA Tour — the ball speed increase from thin-faced titanium drivers as compared to pre-1995 clubs is about 5 mph. This increase, not considering launch angle and spin rate, translates to an additional 10 to 12 yards from the club alone. That's great for the pros, but what about the rest of us?

The clubhead speed for the average golfer is about 85 mph. Switching to titanium will result in a gain of about 8 to 10 yards when the ball is struck on the sweet spot. One of the problems for average golfers is that we don't hit the ball on the sweet spot so regularly, and so our usual gain will be more like 4 to 5 yards. I'll still take it, along with the 8 to 10 I'll get when I do luck into a center-face hit, but it's not enough to radically change my life.

To increase distance further without trying to swing faster, the ball should be launched higher and with less spin. As a general guide, the following are optimal launch conditions, assuming normal turf conditions (on a drier fairway, you'll want to launch the ball a little lower, on a wet one you need more carry):

Head speed	Launch angle	Spin rate
120 MPH	12 DEGREES	2,200 RPM
100 MPH	13 DEGREES	2,400 RPM
80 MPH	14 DEGREES	2,600 3,000 RPM

No matter how fast you swing, you benefit from the big-headed driver's size, because it is engineered to be more forgiving on mishits, functionally increasing the size of the sweet spot. This element of forgiveness is the reason the manufacturers started making the bigger heads in the first place; springlike effect was a by-product, not an intent.

What driver is right for you? Today they're all big, most of them between 400 and 460 cc in volume. This means that they are all very forgiving (have a large MOI, moment of inertia). Also, all of today's drivers have faces that are thin enough to give the maximum benefit of the springlike or trampoline effect, the COR (coefficient of restitution). From a technological point of view, on these two matters they're all pretty much the same. The decision comes down to looks, loft, and a few other factors like weight distribution for a draw bias if you want that built in.

Loft: What loft is best?

Don't you often find that you perform at least as well with a 3-wood off the tee than a driver? In the 1950s, the "2-wood" was popular, because it had a loft of about 10 degrees and was easier to hit than a persimmon driver, which had a typical loft of 7–9 degrees. Soon, many manufacturers introduced drivers with lofts of 10-plus degrees and eliminated the 2-wood from their product lines.

Today, 3-woods perform better than drivers for a large percentage of golfers because we can launch the ball higher, and the increased loft provides more backspin, which in turn reduces the effect of the same sidespin that leads to hooks and slices.

The downside of using a 3-wood is that you don't get the same trampoline effect you do from a big driver, but you do get the higher launch angle that's important at less than PGA Tour swing speeds. Fortunately, today you can get some of both worlds by shopping for a driver with 12 or even 13 degrees of loft. Some manufacturers will even sell you a driver with about 15 degrees of loft, though you may have to go out of your way to ask about it. This is a good option for golfers with a swing speed of 75 mph or less, and is often marketed as a "senior driver." If you swing at 85 mph or less, you should think about a loft of at least 12 degrees; only when your clubhead speed gets to 90 mph or more should you think about going below 12.

Remember that loft is your friend, and that the longer the ball stays on the trampoline-like face, the less spin it will get; combining this with today's low-spin balls and you should be able to use a 12-degree driver to hit shots that fly higher and stay straighter, most likely with no loss of distance.

Shafts. The shaft is the connection between the grip and the clubhead, and its only purpose is to make sure that the head is presented to the ball correctly and at the desired speed. Once impact has begun, the shaft may as well be severed from the head for all the influence it has on the flight of the ball. The inertia of the head takes over once contact has been made, and if the clubhead is going to twist during impact, it will do so around its own center of gravity, with no reference to the axis of the shaft. This is true no matter what manufacturers try to tell you about the magic qualities of their shaft — and it truly would have to be magic to have any effect.

(This sounds like a radical statement, but in fact you already know that it's true. When you hit the ball away from the center of the face towards the toe, you've seen that the ball flies with a slight draw. If the hit is off center towards the heel, the result is a fade. If the clubhead twisted around the shaft instead of around its own center of gravity, both these mishits would fly the same way.)

A shaft that has low torque (two or three degrees) is not going to affect the direction the ball leaves the face of the club. It may help you get the face to the ball at the correct angle, but not to any extent that you're likely to notice and certainly not to a degree that justifies the price some manufacturers charge for such shafts. A $50 graphite shaft is fine for most everybody. I do not believe that tinkering with the shaft away from standard is worthwhile, so long as you've gotten the correct flex.

On the sales floor, the club stands there with a standard shaft, varying only by flex. The manufacturer wouldn't put this shaft in the club if he didn't believe it would make the club perform its best for the vast majority. If you feel your needs require special attention — if you would never sink to buying a shirt off the shelf or a suit off the rack — they will be willing to sell you something that lets you feel important but makes very little difference to your game, unless your handicap is five or less. Until then, improving the consistency of your sweet-spot contact will do far more for you than worrying about adjusting your kick-point. (And even then, I recommend this kind of tinkering only when you've tried everything else in terms of ball position and swing plane to get the trajectory you desire. A low kick-point means the shaft is a little more flexible toward the tip, which generally helps increase the launch angle; the opposite is true for the high kick-point. You'll pay in the neighborhood of $300 for the high-end shafts and this kind of adjustment, which will make very little difference unless you're certain you're hitting the sweet spot time after time.)

In deciding on the proper flex for you, put aside the notion that Real Golfers Go X-Stiff. Yes, the pros use X or Double-X shafts; that's as relevant to your golf game as Shaquille O'Neal's 16 EEEE shoe size is to your jump shot. You want a shaft that feels right to you, that lets you feel where the clubhead is throughout your swing. I believe that the majority of us should play with more flexible shafts than we do. If you use a shaft that's too stiff, one that only works well when you swing it really hard, you'll be fighting it most of the time and won't develop the confidence you need to become consistent. We all intuitively know that a broomstick is too stiff, and a fishing rod is too flexible for a golf club; somewhere in between lies the right shaft for you.

Instead of starting with the stiffest possible shaft and working your way down until one feels okay, you should start on the more flexible side and work your way towards stiffer shafts. Your final result may surprise you, but physics has no ego, and the best shots may come from a shaft that's more flexible than you expected.

A stiff shaft will generally hit the ball with a lower trajectory, but if it's too stiff for you you'll lose feel and the ball will tend to go right. A more flexible shaft allows you to time the swing more effectively, and thus gain a little increase in head speed. Yes, a more flexible shaft will send the ball left if you try to kill your drive, but generally nothing works well under those conditions. There's a reason most golf instructors tell you to swing at no more than 75–80 percent of your strength: the longest shots always come from the middle of the clubface.

In general, if you swing the clubhead at 90 mph or above, you can consider an S (stiff) flex; anything less than this and you should stick to Regular flex, and if your swing speed is below 80 mph you may well benefit from an A flex. Don't let ego get involved here, any more than it should with your shoe size.

As for the shaft length, fifty years ago the standard length was 43 inches. Gary Player used a 44-inch driver in his prime. Tiger Woods used a 43½ -inch steel-shafted driver to win his first several majors. This is shorter than average, which is now about 44½ inches on the PGA Tour. I'm 6-foot-3 in my golf shoes, and I prefer a 44-inch driver for maximum distance and accuracy. Though most manufacturers put 45-inch (or longer) shafts in their titanium drivers, I'd recommend no more than 44 inches for most men of unexceptional height. (For most people, a few inches more or less in average height generally will be balanced by their having longer or shorter arms.) A longer shaft means a longer swing arc, which normally means more speed and thus distance, all things being equal — but all things are never equal, and a slightly shorter shaft will give you more control, which may well give you greater distance as your confidence leads to better swings. Insist on a 44-inch shaft; this will be the hardest request for a salesperson to satisfy, but don't give up — a shorter shaft will always lead to more hits on the sweet spot. A 9-iron is always easier to hit than a 4-iron.

If you're considering shortening your shaft on an existing club, go to the range and choke down on the grip to see how it works. The grip will be a little smaller in this position, and this might affect the test a little bit; shortening the shaft by an inch will also decrease the swingweight and will make the shaft feel a little stiffer. If you want to counteract these changes for purposes of this test, add a little lead tape to the back center part of the head. The results should give you a good idea of the benefit of making this change.

Graphite or steel? The first thing to consider is that a reasonably good graphite shaft will cost you on average about $40 or more apiece. Steel shafts cost less than $10, with newer lightweight steel shafts running about $15.

The main difference between graphite and steel shafts is that graphite is lighter. Changing from steel to graphite will let you use less energy while swinging the club at the same speed, giving you greater control. I generally recommend that female golfers and seniors try graphite or lightweight steel in their iron clubs, and all golfers should use graphite in their woods and even hybrids.

Some male golfers who try to hit the ball too hard — that is, most of us — may lose some of the advantages graphite has to offer;

they'd be better off swinging a little easier for greater control instead of going for increased head speed with their same old erratic swing. The lighter shaft will let them swing even harder, but this won't lead to better shots if it doesn't come with greater accuracy. I would advise them to forget about the potential increase of 5 to 7 yards in distance and to swing slower in a quest for control. I should mention that I have never been able to follow this advice myself, and I don't really expect you to, either.

If you switch from steel to graphite using your existing club head, it will feel lighter and the swingweight will decrease. You'll have to get used to this difference, but remember that the shaft doesn't hit the ball, and the clubhead's weight is unchanged. If you can't get comfortable with the difference, you may want to add some lead tape to the center back part of the head to return to the overall swingweight you're used to. (When manufacturers offer graphite shafted irons, they often make the shaft ½ inch longer than its steel counterpart to maintain the overall swingweight without having to change the head weight; this makes it a little harder for you to control but there is an increase in distance. I am not sure that this is always a good trade-off.)

The Magic 20 Yards. If you have a club with a COR at or near the 0.83 limit, and your clubhead speed is 85 to 100 mph, and you launch the ball at about 13 degrees with a spin rate of between 2,500 and 3,000 rpm, and someone tries to tell you that they have a legal (conforming) driver that will hit the ball 20 yards farther for you, don't believe him. The only way you're going to gain extra distance if you already have the launch conditions above is by increasing clubhead speed through improved swing technique or physical conditioning. If you don't yet launch the ball at these optimum conditions, take some lessons and practice, practice, practice. Ben Hogan said the secret is in the dirt. Looking for it there still works; always has, always will.

To sum up. (1) If you haven't bought a driver in the last five years, do so. Big heads with thin titanium faces give you a definite edge in COR and MOI — springlike effect and forgiveness. (2) Make sure the COR is close to 0.83; as long as you're getting the trampoline boost, you may as well go for the legal maximum. (3) Head size between 400 and 460 cc will give the best performance in distance and accuracy. If you're a very low handicapper; 400 cc is plenty; you're not hitting off-center often enough for the additional forgiveness to make much difference. (4) Look for loft of 12 degrees or more if your swing speed — like most people's — is below 90 mph. You may want to go as high as 15 degrees if your swing is less than 75 mph. Ask to have the loft measured in the shop, as manufacturers used to mark their clubs with a number lower than the actual loft, for marketing reasons. If your swing speed is over 90 mph, consider a 10-degree or lower driver. (5) Find a shaft that's comfortable. Feel you're in control of the clubhead throughout your swing. When testing, start with a more flexible shaft, and move towards the stiffer ones rather than the other way around. Forty-four inches is a good length for most drivers, and you want graphite shafts in all your woods.

Have a Ball

The choice of ball can affect your results, but as with clubs, the differences between various top brands are much slighter than the variance in our ability to hit a consistent shot.

Even some very low handicap golfers find it a little difficult to tell the differences between, for example, the Pro V1 and the Pro V1x or other top brands. They may be able to distinguish between the performance around the greens of the less-expensive hard-covered low-spin balls and the premium balls, but even these differences may elude those of us who are less skilled, and we certainly won't be able to take advantage of them.

When you reach the skill level where you can impart a variety of spins on your pitch and chip shots and want a specific trajectory for your 280-yard drives, that's the time to pay upwards of $50 a dozen for a premium ball. Until then, you're mostly paying for vanity and for the pleasure that another golfer will feel when he fishes your ball out of a hazard.

In fact, if you don't hit the ball at clubhead speeds of more than 85–90 mph, the softer-core balls will probably provide more distance, as well as adequate-to-good performance around the greens.

If, however, you believe that a specific ball is the best for you and you have confidence playing it, then use it, because there's no substitute for confidence and belief. That confidence is worth more than any performance characteristic that has been built into a golf ball in the past ten years.

Nearly all golf balls today are very good; this was not the case in the past. For twenty-six years I directed testing of all the golf balls used in competition, and we found that some famous makes of golf balls varied more from ball to ball than most brands varied from each other. To make sure that the balls being distributed to Tour players were the same as those originally submitted for the conforming list, I tested balls taken directly from the Tour reps. Because only a few players were using the MacGregor ball in 1977, I had to ask Jack Nicklaus and some others directly for samples to test. Jack gave me several sleeves from his bag, and we learned through testing with a mechanical golfer that the balls were so poor — their performance was so inconsistent — that I'm convinced he would have won several more majors if he'd used a different, better ball. (I eventually told him so, in 2000.) Today, ball production has improved enormously so such variation is almost impossible to find; nonetheless, there are some design differences from ball to ball.

Construction. The standard premium ball for nearly a century had a liquid center wrapped with rubber threads, a concept pioneered with the Haskell ball in 1898 that replaced the solid gutta-percha. These balls performed well for the professionals, especially when they didn't have to pay for them, but amateurs found that mishits would often leave a "smile" on the surface of the ball, affecting its performance. Ball makers tried to come up with a more durable, less expensive alternative, introducing a new solid ball — totally solid, one piece — in 1965, and in 1970 tried a two-piece ball with a cover placed over a solid core. The professionals were not converts, because the balls did not spin as much off wedges and other short irons as the wound soft-covered "balata" balls did. (These balls were known as balata even though real balata had not been used on the cover for many years. The cover was a mix of materials that had similar properties but were easier to come by and lasted longer than balata.)

The pros did like the extra distance the harder solid balls gave them, as the balls were slightly faster, launched higher and had less spin, but were unwilling to give up the control around the greens. The solution, first conceived and patented by Spalding in 1984, was a multilayered ball, with which some professionals had success in the mid 1990s. These two- and three-piece balls — essentially a solid ball with a soft cover came out from Spalding under the Strata label, and Mark O'Meara used it to win two major championships in 1998.

By 2000, at least five ball companies had introduced multilayer balls that were being used on the PGA Tour.

In late 2000, Titleist brought out the Pro V1. Within weeks of the formal introduction in early 2001, 80 percent of those using Titleist balls (roughly 68 percent of all Tour players) had switched to a multilayered ball. These balls had reasonably hard resilient cores, a thin casing, and a soft thin cover. For the first time, a ball could achieve optimum launch conditions for fast swing speeds (i.e., a high launch and low spin) with a driver, yet spin sufficiently for stopping and control on approach shots to and around the green.

The average golfer had long been able to take advantage of the hard-core/hard-cover two-piece ball for added distance through reduced spin. The Pro V1 married this performance off the tee to improved spin on approaches, but to take advantage of the characteristics you need to be able to hit the ball hard and accurately. At slower speeds, a softer core does a better job of overall performance, which is one reason that senior players in the late 1990s discovered that they did better playing with balls originally designed for women golfers with less powerful swings. (To help assuage the male ego, Precept changed the name of its softest-core ball from Lady to Laddie.)

There is a very clear reason the average golfer should play with a soft-core, hard-covered ball: It produces the maximum distance with reduced spin, so it flies straighter than a high-spinning ball. It won't spin as much off the wedges and short irons, but if you've never caused a ball to back up on the green, the Pro V1 may not do that for you either, and you'll pay a lot of money for performance characteristics your game cannot take advantage of and doesn't need. Most of the major golf ball companies produce some very good (less than premium) balls that most of us ought to try before emptying our wallets.

Dimples: The dimples on a golf ball create a turbulent layer of air at the ball's surface. This combines with the backspin you impart at impact to help the ball fly through the air. A smooth ball would only fly about 140 yards or less, while a dimpled ball will fly 260 yards or more. This was a phenomenon recognized by golfers in the 19th century, who noticed that older, slightly hacked-up balls flew farther than new, smooth ones; ball makers began putting marks in the surface of the ball to take advantage of this effect.

As ball manufacturers came to understand this property more thoroughly, dimple designs became more formal. In the early 1970s there was a dimple race, as marketers trumpeted their favorite fallacious argument, If Many Is Good Then More Is Better. I have seen as few as 252 dimples on a golf ball and as many as 812. The number of dimples is somewhat self-limiting; eventually, a ball with too many dimples behaves much the same as a smooth one. The optimal number of dimples appears to be between 300 and 450, with varying sizes on the same ball.

The USGA has never seriously considered dictating dimple specifications to control performance; it would be difficult to enforce (imagine having to measure and count the dimples on every make of ball) and would limit the ability of manufacturers to create customized products. It's much easier and more effective to measure the overall performance of the ball, rather than specific characteristics such as dimple design.

Compression. Remember compression? Compression is basically a measure of the hardness of a ball (the amount it deforms under a specific load). In the small-core wound-ball days, all balls were designed to have a compression of about 95; some turned out to be 100, and others were 90, 80, or even 70 (these were marketed as ladies' balls). These compression differences were a result of uncontrolled variations in the production process, and the companies used marketing techniques to make potential rejects seem as though they had specific virtues. (The higher compression balls were a little faster at higher impact speeds.)

With today's golf balls, compression is no longer an important consideration, and it's certainly not used to market the product. Some very good balls have a very low compression rating. It's easy to wonder now what the fuss was about.

Temperature. Air temperature has a distinct influence on ball performance. The hotter and more humid the air is, the less dense it is. The lower the density, the less drag resistance there is, but also the less the effective lift. This phenomenon can be seen in airplanes: they find it more difficult to take off on hot, humid days than on cold, dry ones.

Balls will generally carry about two-thirds of a foot farther for every increase of one degree Fahrenheit in temperature. A ten-degree difference gives you about 2 yards of extra carry.

Humidity. Humidity's effects on a performance are not measurable, though we do like to blame decreased distance on muggy days to "heavy air." In fact, on humid days the ball has less lift because the air is actually "lighter" rather than heavier. When there are droplets in the air — when it's raining — then the medium through which the ball is flying can be said to be heavy. But the prime effect that would account for worse performance on muggy days is probably the humidity's effect on our own energy levels.

Lifespan. Balls don't deteriorate much any more. The insides of a modern ball last a lot longer than its cover; the wear and tear on the cover — especially if you hit a few skulled shots, cart paths, or spend some time in the bunkers — will have you tossing your ball into the shag bag long before any significant changes due to age. Balls kept in a dry place for four or five years will see no measurable decrease in distance or performance.

Is it okay to use lost balls you've found during your rounds? If you found it, then it's not lost; if it looks new and has the original brand name on it rather than having been repainted, it should work just fine. A lake, however, is not a dry place; if a ball's been sitting in a pond for several days, there's a good chance that the watery environment will hurt performance. That's why I'd be leery of balls I found buried in the woods; you have no way of knowing how long they've been there or what the weather has been. I'd still put them in the shag bag, though. (And keep in mind Mark Twain's advice that when picking up a lost ball, it is considered only polite to wait until it stops rolling.)

For most of us, golf balls last until we lose them — which, sadly, isn't very long.

The Bottom Line. My advice is to play with any ball you feel performs well for you and enhances your game. This will help you build confidence. But of course, there is the seductive quality of that one shot in fifty when everything comes together — the timing of your swing and all the moving parts are in synch, the planets are all in alignment — and you make perfect contact. Under these circumstances, you'wouldn't want even a single yard or two to come between you and absolute perfection; that's when you'll benefit from a top of the line ball. How much you're willing to spend for that very rare shot and the wonderful experience you derive is a question only you can answer.

To sum up: (1) Try out a variety of golf balls until you find one you like and gain confidence with. Don't change brands too often; when you find a ball you like, stick with it. There are enough variables to contend with in golf without questioning whether your ball is right for you. (2) Choosing a ball has become simpler (believe it or not!). Balls are either two-piece or multilayered. (3) If your handicap is over ten, use a two- or three-piece soft-core ball. The two piece balls have a soft core and a variety of cover hardnesses. The ones with harder covers are considered "distance balls." Those with softer covers provide more spin, but not a noticeable decrease in distance. These balls are also half to one-third the price of the multilayered premium balls. (4) Multilayered balls are good for all golfers, but best for golfers who require sufficient distance off the driver and can control their shots around the green.

THE WHOLE SET

How many clubs should you carry? Do you need the long irons, or are they just taking up space in our bags? What do you really need in the way of club fitting? How many wedges do you need and why? What should you look for in a putter? Are hybrids here to stay?

If you don't know the answers to these questions, you're not alone. There's a whole industry dependent upon making you think you need things you don't. Most golfers are sold on the value of being fitted for a brand new set of customized clubs, when in most cases a standard set of clubs will be just as good. Some companies offer a customized set for every customer and have the ability to make and ship these sets in a matter of forty-eight hours or less — but their data show that up to 80 percent of the requested "customized" specs are, in fact, "standard."

Consider this story told by Butch Harmon in his book, *The Pro: Lessons From My Father About Golf and Life*:

> Tommy Armour, who remained a member at Winged Foot long after he retired from competitive golf, told Dad [Claude Harmon, the pro at Winged Foot] every year that he needed to order 50 sets of Tommy Armour Silver Scot irons and woods, 25 sets with stiff shafts and 25 sets with regular shafts. Then, throughout the year, as Mr. Armour would play with members, they would always ask, "Tommy, what clubs do you think I should play?"
>
> He would put his arm around any member who asked and say, "Tell you what I'm going to do. I'll call the factory this afternoon and order a custom set of clubs that suits your game perfectly. Don't worry about a thing. I'll take care of it."
>
> After the round, Tommy would stick his head in the door of Dad's office and say, "Claude, in two weeks stick a set of regulars in Mr. Smith's bag." Dad sold 50 sets of Tommy Armour Silver Scots every year based on Mr. Armour's "custom-fitting" technique.

The Armour technique worked because nearly all clubs work for most people, and because the major benefit from a fully fitted set is psychological — the belief that it "suits your game perfectly." Unlike the pros, we don't have swings that repeat so precisely that it makes sense to set our idiosyncrasies in steel and graphite. The angle we tweak today may need retweaking tomorrow.

Let's take a hard look at the real story of what's right for you.

Length. The only reason you might need a club that differs from standard length is you differ from average height by more than half a foot. Within the normal range – from 5'4" to 6'4" for men, 4'10½" to 5'9½" for women – the length of your arms generally will compensate for the difference in height for standard clubs.

The average man stands about 5'10", the average woman about 5'4½". However, traditional ladies' clubs have been only one inch shorter than men's standard. This tells us that most people are able to adapt to and successfully use, a standard length without alteration. Standard is good at least 95 percent of the time.

For drivers, a longer club may give us more clubhead speed, but in general, the longer the club, the less you can control a shot with it. (Consider buying a snakebite kit along with the extra-length driver.) An extra-long driver for added power means you'll have to develop a different and flatter swing for this one club — and it's the club that can get you into the most trouble, because you're trying to hit it the farthest. You're much better off with a standard length (preferably 44-inch) driver and maintaining the same swingweight and flex or feel as the rest of your set.

Consider the following: If one precise length is right for your individual game, why would it make sense to have different clubs in your bag differ in length? Your 4-iron isn't the same length as your 8-iron, is it? (Sets with equal length throughout the bag have been tried a number of times over the last fifty years, and their failure to capture the market shows that the principle doesn't work.) If you're of average height and during the fitting process the fitter suggests that your new 6-iron — the club used most often for measurement — should be a half-inch longer than standard because you're stooping too much to be effective, won't you have the exact same problem with your new 7-iron? This is not to say that you won't do very well with your new half-inch-longer clubs; we are very adaptable creatures, and a half inch is very little difference. The question is, are you doing better because of the half inch or in spite of it? If it makes no difference, why go through the hassle and expense of the fitting for small differences that may require changing weights, etc.?

I make this argument only to reinforce the fact that a standard-length set should be just fine, unless you are abnormally different from the standard-sized human being.

Swingweight and natural frequency. The term "swingweight" is a guideline for matching clubs. It relates to the overall weight of the components of the club when balanced statically on a fulcrum. It is based on the amount of weight that must be attached to the butt end of a club to make it balance on a sharp edge positioned 14 inches from that end.

The concept is a fine one as far as it goes, but its practical applications are more uncertain. The problem is that the measure is a precise one, but our realities are messy. A dirty club head might have enough soil in its grooves to change the balance and alter the swingweight by a couple of points. Placing a glove on the grip end of the balanced club will obviously change the balance and thus the swingweight measurement by as much as five points; wearing or not wearing a wristwatch throws off the effective swingweight when you use the club as well.

We know from our experience that such minor matters won't affect our swing noticeably. So is swingweight of any importance? Yes, but only if the shaft and grip weights are the same and only the head weight is altered. It is best used in conjunction with overall weight.

Standard swingweights for men are about D0-D2 and about C6-C8 for women. If we increase the length of the club by a half-inch with everything else the same, this will increase the swingweight by about three points, which is about the slightest change that a golfer is able to feel. This might not affect their performance, but a manufacturer will sometimes try to maintain the same swingweight on a shorter club by altering the head weight or putting a little extra weight in the tip end of the shaft; this will make the scale turn out the way it's supposed to, but does nothing of consequence to help the golfer.

In general, checking swingweight would matter more if there were a wide variation in the balance of clubs being manufactured for a single set, but with today's quality controls this isn't much of an issue.

There is another method of matching a set of clubs, called the natural frequency method, which is a dynamic method of matching (as opposed to the static measurement used in swingweight) and more related to how the club feels when you swing it. The frequency method is based on clamping the club at the grip end and plucking it so it oscillates; the number of oscillations (in cycles per minute) is used as the measure.

Imagine a long carving knife that is wedged into a crack in a picnic table and plucked. It will vibrate, and the number of vibrations is the frequency of that knife when embedded at a particular depth. In order to increase the frequency — to make it play a higher note, if you want to think of it that way — you have to do one of several things: embed it deeper; decrease the weight of the knife handle that's sticking up in the air; or increase the stiffness of the blade. Similarly, a club's frequency can be increased by decreasing the length, lessening the head weight, or stiffening the shaft. This makes more sense than the swingweight system for a balancing method that simulates "feel." Combining the two may be even better.

Swingweight and frequency are another area in which the standard measures will work just fine for the overwhelming majority of golfers. When your touch has developed to such an extent that you can feel slight variations and take advantage of the differences, then you might want to consider having your clubs matched by the frequency method. Such virtuosi exist, but most of them are playing on Tour. Don't get carried away with swingweights; with a big enough scale and by moving weight around, I can bring a telephone pole down to a D2 swingweight. Another method of matching is by the MOI of the system about the grip axis, and I am sure you will hear more about this in the future.

The factors that matter. The two areas where you should pay attention are shaft flex and lie angle; these are the most important parts of selecting the right club for you. I discussed shaft flex in the context of drivers, earlier in this chapter. Here's the skinny on lie angle.

Lie angle describes how the clubhead is angled to the shaft and is measured from the sole or bottom of the club. This angle has a direct effect on the flight of the ball, assuming you've made a good swing.

The lie angle is ultimately dependant upon your swing plane, and again, standard is good enough for most golfers. You should only consider altering your lie angle if you know your swing is sound and your ball flight indicates that there's a problem. If the lie angle is too flat, the ball will generally go right of the target; if it's too upright, the ball will generally go left.

114 · Frank Thomas

To test your lie angle, hit balls and observe the flight path. If it is consistently left or right, use a lie board to see if the lie angle is the cause. Most golf professionals have a lie board, which is a hard plastic or wooden board from which you hit the ball. Pressure-sensitive tape is applied to the sole of the club, and when it makes contact with the board it leaves a mark that shows where the contact took place.

If the mark on the tape is in the middle of the sole, then lie angle is not your problem and you may need to work on your swing. If the mark is towards the toe or the heel, your lie angle may need adjusting. For markings on the toe, the lie has to be made more upright; toward the heel, make the lie more flat.

Adjustments to the lie can be made with a bending machine that many golf professionals or local club makers will have. Don't change the lie by more than four degrees, as this may weaken the club in the hosel area. Also, be aware that most woods have a short hosel that is not designed to allow for such adjustments. The lower the loft, the less important the lie angle is, so this should not be a major problem.

Changing your lie angle won't compensate for fundamental swing problems, but it's something to look into if your flight-path errors run in the same consistent direction.

Grips. The grip may be the one area where you should consider changing from standard sizes and materials, as this is your only connection to the club. You have to feel comfortable when you grip the club.

In choosing a grip size, grasp the club with your left hand (assuming you're right-handed), making sure the middle and ring fingers don't dig into the meaty portion of your hand at the base or heel of the left thumb. If the fingertips just touch this portion of the hand, then the grip size should be just right.

There are many grip materials of different textures, and you should try several to figure out which ones you prefer. Most grips today do well in wet weather, which was not the case years ago. You definitely don't want the club slipping in your downswing.

You may want to wear a glove to improve your hold on the club, which will generally prevent you from squeezing down too hard just to keep the club from slipping.

Iron clubheads. This is probably the area where most golfers make their biggest mistakes.

There are basically two types of iron clubheads: blades and cavity-backs. The blade club is rounded on the back and is used by the best players in the world. Club designers, who know that we don't hit the ball consistently on the sweet spot, have designed a cavity into the back of the club to distribute the weight around the perimeter of the head to make it forgiving of mishits. (Chapter three has a discussion of the development of the first cavity backs.) This form of repositioning of weight has the effect of increasing the moment of inertia, and it makes our mishits work out better. Such clubs help us enjoy the game more, though some of us are still confused by the fact that the best players prefer blades and we think maybe we should too.

Truth is, the best players have a level of control we can only barely imagine. They rarely miss the sweet spot and at will can change their swings to produce a fade or draw or other variation of spin. The cavity-back clubs — certainly those with the highest MOI — reduce their ability to take advantage of their skills, as some mediocre shots feel similar to the good ones. We don't have their skills, and when we present the clubhead to the ball at a slightly different angle than normal, it's rarely deliberate and rarely pleasant. We need the help the increased MOI gives us; they don't.

Over the last thirty years, irons have become more playable for two reasons: both the increase in MOI, and the change in the location of the center of gravity (c.g.), which has moved down, back, and closer to being opposite the center of the clubface than was the case in the mid 1960s. This lowered and centered c.g. makes it easier to get the ball up in the air; a similar effect makes hybrid clubs, introduced in the last five years, easier to hit than long irons. Only the trained eye can determine where the center of gravity is located through visual inspection, and therefore what clubs are more forgiving and helpful than others. Clubs can now be classified on the basis of c.g. location and MOI into six different categories of playability, ranging from Ultra-Game Improvement (the maximum forgiveness) to Player Classic (for experts only).

The type of iron you need is somewhat dependent on your skill level. The better players can use any clubs, but will generally choose from the Conventional or Classic categories, while most golfers should be looking at Ultra-Game Improvement or Super-Game Improvement categories. These clubs get the ball up quicker, launching it higher with a little more spin, and are forgiving of mishits off the sweet spot.

There are many clubs that don't cost a lot and still perform very well, so look around. Most of the clubs categorized and listed on our website are of good quality and well worth considering.

The Bottom Line. You don't have to be "fitted" in the formal sense with minor adjustments to length, swingweight, frequency, or shaft kick points, etc., but you may want to pay attention to shaft flex and lie angle. Other types of adjustment are a costly way to achieve a mostly psychological effect.

Find the most comfortable and playable clubs you can, taking advantage of the game-improvement characteristics of modern irons without worrying too much about too many details. Standard clubs will do fine until you're consistently shooting in the mid to low 70s. If you reach that point and feel your equipment is holding you back, then it's time to fine-tune your equipment further. Until then, work on improving *you* instead of your clubs.

HYBRIDS

The hybrid is not a new idea, but it has recently taken the industry by storm. The first of the most recent popular versions of the hybrid was the Rescue by TaylorMade. Its ancestors were the Ginty and Baffler. These wooden clubs, when introduced, were considered utility clubs, i.e., not part of the set. They were used from semirough conditions and odd lies, but were also found to be very effective from good fairway lies and easier to hit than the long irons. They were more accurate than the fairway woods because they had shorter shafts.

The Rescue's success in the late '90s started a flurry of activity in this newly accepted club once the professionals started using them, and therefore they were no longer considered an "old man's club." Because something had to go in the set if this club was to have a place, the long irons became the victims.

The hybrid club is now close to being perfected, and it definitely has a place in every serious golfer's bag.

The reason it works differently than a fairway wood is that its MOI is slightly less, it has a low and rearward positioned center of gravity (c.g.) but not as far back as the fairway wood, and in most cases it is much shorter than the comparable fairway wood, by about 2 to 2.5 inches.

Because of these differences, the hybrid generally causes a lower ball flight than the fairway wood, while being more accurate because of the difference in length. It's easier to control but shorter in distance than the fairway wood of similar loft.

As compared to the long irons of similar loft, the hybrid is more accurate, easier to control, and more forgiving because of its higher MOI and the low and rearward positioning of its center of gravity. It will hit the ball a little higher and farther than an iron with the same loft. It is also about ½ to 1 inch longer than the iron.

The shaft flex of the hybrid should be the same as the iron it is replacing. If you select a graphite shaft (not a bad choice), be aware that with every graphite shaft the length is increased by a half-inch compared to the steel counterpart to compensate for the lighter shaft weight and to maintain the same swingweight.

The Bottom Line: Every serious golfer should have at least one hybrid in his bag. It should be about ½ to 1 inch longer than the iron it is replacing and have a shaft flex similar to that iron.

To make room, you will need to drop one of your fairway woods (probably the 5- or 7-wood) and/or the 3- or 4-iron. The 4-hybrid (22 to 24 degree loft, depending on the make) will not allow you to hit that "low-under-the-branches" shot as well as the regular 4-iron, so it may be a good idea to keep this club in the bag for when you need a low iron trajectory.

If you are going to get two hybrids and presently have a 3-iron, then go for the 21 and 24 degree and dump the 3-iron and a wood.

I am sure we will see hybrids included as part of the regular set of clubs relatively soon. The introduction and acceptance of this club is one of the best advances made in the game in the last ten years;

golfers at all levels have benefited from its being easier to hit with control and accuracy than the clubs it replaces.

WEDGES

The history of the wedge is long and has taken some interesting turns in the last several decades.

The wedge evolved from the clubs called niblicks, which had large heads and the most loft of any of the early iron clubs. They were used to get the ball up in the air quickly to clear the face of a bunker or to get over any other obstacles between you and the hole.

The club we think of as a wedge now was primarily a utility club developed to help get the ball out of the sand. Gene Sarazen is credited with having created the first true sand wedge in the 1930s, by welding a metal flange to the bottom of a niblick to help it slide through the sand without digging in too deeply. This addition to the sole of the clubhead, which we now call "bounce," meant that the back of the sole was lower than the club's leading edge. Today we talk about the angle of the bounce, that angle that runs from front to back when a sand wedge is in the normal address position. Fourteen degrees is a common bounce angle for sand wedges, and it's what I'd recommend for your primary bunker-shot club.

There is a problem with bounce, however. The same attribute that brings the club back to the surface when you're hitting from sand can cause you to skull a shot when you're hitting from a firm surface like hardpan or a tight fairway. When the specialized sand wedge took the place of the niblick, players found they still needed a club they could use from the fairway and rough, and so the pitching wedge became popular . Unlike the sand wedge, which is viewed as a utility club and not an integral part of most matched sets, the pitching wedge is the continuation of the line of clubs that begins with the 1-iron and proceeds through the 9-iron. Its function and technique are not substantially different from the short irons that lead to it, but with a greater loft it will get the ball into the air faster.

For many years, the pitching wedge and sand wedge sat together at the short end of the club rack, the two of them sufficient to handle nearly any task with a little manipulation — opening the face to get the ball up faster, closing a little to get more run on an approach shot. In the 1980s, however, with green speeds increasing, some short-game masters experimented with even higher-lofted irons than the 55 or 56 degrees that had become standard for the sand wedge. The lob wedge (usually 60 degrees, though today it can go as high as 64 degrees) became popular for pitching the ball high and stopping it fast from lies near the green. Since those lies could include some firm turf conditions, the lob wedge generally does not have much bounce on them, which makes them a little dicey from the sand. Pros like Phil Mickelson can do wonderful things with them out of bunkers, but such artists could probably use a 7-iron from greenside sand and still make the ball sit, dance, and sing an aria from *Aida*. For the rest of us, a 60-degree wedge became a sign that we were serious about our short games, so long as no one actually asked us to practice with it. It also gave us the option to hit spectacular high-lofted shots with a full swing from a greenside lie — at least, on those one-in-three occasions when we didn't drill the ball into somebody's backyard instead.

The 60-degree wedge is a response to the triumph of the American-style golf course, where the greens are often ringed with bunkers the golfer must pitch over. Anyone who has visited the links of Scotland

and tried to hit his lob wedge soon discovers the extent of its folly; there is almost always a better, lower, safer alternative to hitting a high lob shot off firm links turf. It is also a rare example of a club designed to hit the ball shorter than the club it augments; most clubs are sold on the basis of their additional length. This truth has led, in a roundabout way, to the most recent development in wedges, or at least in wedge names.

The competition to sell golf clubs has been around for a long time. If you're a manufacturer, it is up to you to prove that your wares are better than those of your competitors. One way to do this is to demonstrate that your 5-iron, say, hits the ball farther than someone else's 5-iron. The laws of physics, however, do not allow for miraculous transformations; if your clubhead weighs the same as someone else's and is swung at the same speed and has the same loft and impact is made at the same point on the clubface, the ball is going to travel the same distance. How do you make your 5-iron hit the ball farther?

Easy. You cheat.

Maybe "cheat" is too strong a word. After all, there is no governing body standing over manufacturers and ordaining the loft specifications of a given numbered club. The numbers placed on a club are a convenience, not sworn testimony. If I give my 5-iron 3 to 4 degrees less loft than the generally accepted standard, so that its face is at the angle we usually associate with a 4-iron instead of a 5, a solidly struck ball will go farther. In the early 1970s, some foreign manufacturers started changing the lofts of their clubs by these 3 to 4 degrees without changing the club number, and once this happened the unwritten standard of lofts was out the window. All manufacturers followed suit, and delofted their clubs — and once they were delofting, why stop at 3 or 4 degrees? Some went as far as 6 degrees or so. Golfers were hitting their 5-irons (and 6-irons and 7-irons and so on) farther than ever before. In reality, we were simply adjusting our club choices on their approach shots, but that's not how it felt to our marketing-receptive brains.

With all the lofts in the set changing, the 1-iron became even more unhittable than it had been before, and before long it and even the 2-iron (which now had the same loft as the 1-iron) were becoming extinct. *Roll over and one fell out/And then they all rolled over again and another one fell out.* But on the bottom end, the sand wedge refused to roll, staying in the same spot without changing its loft at all, remaining steadfast at about 55 degrees.

The pitching wedge, however, was caught up in the loft deflation, getting stronger along with all the other irons in the set. The PW was originally around 51 degrees, but today it's more like 46 degrees, the loft of a former 9-iron. It is still general practice to have about 4 degrees between the lofts of consecutive short clubs (i.e., 8-iron, 9-iron, PW). The delofting thus created a gap of about 9 or 10 degrees between the PW and the SW, depending on the set.

As nature abhors a vacuum, golfers and manufacturers abhor a gap, and they have now filled it with the gap wedge, a newly designated club with a loft between 50 and 52 degrees and a bounce angle of about 8 degrees. In general, this gap wedge will hit the ball about 10 to 15 yards shorter than your PW; it's primarily used from fairway and rough, not from sand, so it doesn't need the bounce associated with the sand wedge. In reality, it's pretty much the club the pitching wedge used to be, but now that strengthened and lengthened club is considered an integral part of a set of irons, and the GW is a utility club to be added separately.

The gap wedge fills an essential function resulting from the changes in club specifications over the last thirty to forty years. I definitely recommend you add one to your bag to fill that space between the PW and SW. As for the lob wedge, this is a more personal decision. Before the development of the LW, golfers adjusted on short shots by opening the face of their sand wedges or PW; this is still an option, though the 14-degree bounce on a modern SW makes this dicey from hardpan or tight lies. If you decide you do want a lob wedge for close greenside pitches, make sure to get one with no more than 6 to 8 degrees of bounce and that the bounce is rounded from the front to the back of the club. And practice, practice, practice with it: The club face may look as big as a snow shovel to you as you look down on it, but from the ball's point of view it's as slender as a blade that can either run completely under the ball without touching it if the ball is sitting up in deep rough, or can slice right into the belly of the ball with its leading edge if the turf is tight.

The Putter and the Putting Stroke

The putter is probably the most important club in the bag. If that statement surprises you, ask yourself: Is there another club that you use on average twice a hole? There are more styles of putter than of any other type of club, and you should pay more attention to your choice here than you do for any other club in your bag.

Length: The length of your putter for the traditional method of putting (i.e., not the long putter or the belly putter) should be such that, when you're bent over in a comfortable address position with your eyes approximately over the ball and your spine at about a 45-degree angle, the end of the grip doesn't extend more than one inch above the upper hand when you hold your arms straight. This converts to a length of about 34 inches for most men between 5' 6" and 6' 3", with 5' 10" being the average height for an American male, and 30 to 32 inches for most women.

The key here is that your arms be relatively straight at address when you are ready to make a stroke and that you be comfortable, with your eyes approximately over the ball. In this position you should not be choking down on the putter grip.

Head: I highly recommend that the putter head be a mallet style, i.e., about 3 inches deep (from face to back) and about 4½ inches from toe to heel. The center of gravity should be close to the center of the head and as low as possible. The weight distribution should be such that it has a high MOI to minimize the effect of impacts towards the toe and heel, as well as contact above or below the sweet spot. This last point may seem like a small factor, since the ball is sitting on the green, and it's almost impossible to contact it too high on the face. However, it is possible to hit it towards the bottom, either by mistake or intentionally when the ball is sitting against the short rough cut at the edge of the green, or to hit the ball on the upstroke, and a blade putter (or one with heel-toe weighting only) will lose effectiveness and distance control from the up and down off-center contact, costing you both feel and consistency.

Sole: The sole of the putter should curve gently from toe to heel to accommodate differences in green surface at address, as well as small differences in each golfer's address position (lie angle) which is generally about 72 degrees. Variations in lie angle will be very small if the putter is fitted to the correct length based on the guidelines above.

Balance: The putter should be face balanced, which mean that when the putter is balanced on the arms of a chair, the face points directly upward. This will help eliminate unwanted small forces in the forward part of the putting stroke that tend to rotate the face off-line. Face balancing also helps in the overall balance of the putter during a stroke .

Weight: The head weight of the putter should be about 350 grams (12 1/3 ounces). Some players may want a head as heavy as 380 grams, but a heavier head doesn't necessarily make for a more efficient stroke; it's purely a matter of what feels right to you.

Swingweight: There's no reason to even consider swingweight when it come to putters or try to match the swingweight of a putter to that of the other clubs in your bag. The only reason this would make a difference is if you intend to take a full swing with your putter. About the only time most golfers do this is in preparation for flinging it into a lake.

Shaft location: A personal thing. Center-shafted putters are becoming more popular, but if you prefer to see more of the head and its lines, then a heel-mounted, bent-shafted putter should work just as well. Some golfers like a putter to have an offset head, i.e., the axis of the shaft is slightly ahead of the face; this can help you position the ball a little farther back in your stance, if that's important to you. Again, this is a matter of personal preference, not general performance.

The Bottom Line: If you have the correct length and head design, and you've found your personal preferences in shaft location and weight, you've got everything you need to start making more putts. So let's look at the putting stroke.

Putting Stroke: Unless you have developed the yips at some point, I recommend that you use a regular length putter rather than a long or belly putter. The long putter restricts your natural ability to make a consistent stroke for all distances and tends to decrease the all-important feel aspect of putting. Gaining a feel for distance is crucial to being a good putter. This feel is somewhat instinctive in nature, and it requires all your moving parts to express themselves freely if you want to translate what you see into what you need to do. This does not mean that all the parts capable of moving should be moving, but you should be in charge of their not moving (if this makes any sense).

As an experiment, try to throw a ball underhanded to someone 3 feet away, and then 23 feet away. First do so with no restrictions of any kind; then put your elbow and wrist joints into a splint and try the same throws again. Until you practice a lot and get used to the unnatural restricted feeling, your distance dispersion will be very erratic. The stroke with a long putter — anchored against your body with one hand and pushed with the other — eliminates some potential errors but does so at the cost of the freedom that creates feel. You probably won't need as many hours of practice with a conventional stroke to develop the control that lets you use your natural instincts to judge distance and speed.

We have trained and are working with some very good tour players and some not so good golfers at our Putting Studio near Orlando, using high tech video and kinematic analysis, preshot techniques as well as some advanced sports psychology to help them develop confidence and to have good reason for it. Saving strokes on the green means a couple of dollars and pride to some but means a living to others.

Every club requires you to control both direction and distance, but none of them call for as much fine accuracy as the putter. The target isn't a fairway or a green, but rather a hole that's just 4¼ inches in diameter, which you're trying to hit from as far away as 50 feet or more. (The equivalent target for a 250-yard drive would be a fairway 1.77 yards wide.) Also, very few putts per round are the same distance or have exactly the same break.

When you make a putting stroke, you are using your arms, which can bend at the elbow; your shoulders, which should be swinging in unison; wrists that should be kept locked but can be very floppy and will bend or twist if you let them; and a posture that should stay motionless but which tends to sway with the stroke — all this to hit putts that have plenty of variables of their own to deal with.

These are the degrees of freedom we are trying to control when we hit a putt. We want to groove our stroke so that it delivers the clubface to the ball consistently, varying only by the speed that will determine distance. If you could lock your shoulders, your arms, and your wrists together so these create one single unit with the putter and let the putter swing like a pendulum from a fixed point around your neck, you would eliminate many of the variables that can throw our strokes off-line.

This is the appeal of the long or belly putter: It minimizes or eliminates the chances of unwanted up-and-down movement and the undue wrist rotation of the clubhead and removes the variable axis of rotation due to the wrist flick movements because the axis is located in your belly or on your chest. The arms are the only moving parts. This is a very efficient method of putting if we are only concerned about direction.

If you have tried everything but can't get rid of the jerky movements during the putting stroke that we call the yips, then by all means give the long or belly putter a try. The length is dependent on the style, but 45 to 52 inches is the general range for the long putter, and 40 to 44 inches is best for the belly-putting style. Again, your putting style, posture, and body shape will dictate the final fitted length.

The lie angle for long putters should be 79 degrees (80 is the legal limit), but for the belly putter a lie of 72 degrees is good.

The head weight for the long putter will usually be a bit heavier than a conventional putter, close to 380 grams (13.4 ounces) in order for it to feel comfortable; the belly putter can run from 350 to 380, depending on your preference.

There is always the risk that the USGA may some day try to ban the long and belly putter, based on that group's unpredictable and very questionable rulings of late. If that happens, you'll have to go back to the conventional technique and style. I recognize that the putting method employed by people using long putters is an improvement in efficiency, but some believe it is not "traditional." I know it is more efficient, as anytime you can eliminate degrees of freedom you simultaneously eliminate the associated errors. I must admit that when the decision was made by the USGA I was among those in favor of limiting the length of a putter. My feelings are now that I would still rather see a golfer using a conventional style of putting and forgo the Band-Aid approach of using the long putter. But the bottom line is, if it does what it should do and allows you to exhibit your potential, then go for it.

I personally use a conventional but extremely well-designed mallet-headed model – a Frankly Frog, naturally.

CHAPTER SIX: By the Rules

The oldest Rules of Golf that we know about were set down in the middle of the 18th century, though people had been playing the game for hundreds of years before that. None of these original (written) rules placed any restrictions on the game's equipment. That's because everybody knew what a ball was, and everybody knew what a club was, and that was all anybody needed to know. Maybe that's all we need to know.

Today there is an extensive and increasingly detailed body of rules dealing with the game's implements and balls. Dimensions are specified in excruciating detail; test procedures are described for the benefit of would-be manufacturers and their sure-to-be lawyers. As the rules have become more exacting, they've also become more subject to debate and concern: Do they do what we want them to do? And what do we want them to do, anyway?

When it comes to equipment, I've found there are three general objectives for creating a regulation: the Traditional objective (the desire to protect traditions of the game), the Sameness objective (to ensure that all competitors are on a roughly equal footing), and the Challenge objective (to make certain that technological innovations do not reduce or eliminate the skill the game requires). Some rules might fall into more than one of these categories, but most are aimed at accomplishing at least one of these purposes.

The Challenge objective has led to a great deal of debate in recent years, based in excessive concern that the professionals are making the game too easy and their progress (especially in distance) must be reined in. Fear is a frequent substitute for understanding, and this seems to be the case here as well. Limits have been placed on equipment that are wholly unnecessary, the equivalent of setting a speed limit of 95 mph when automobiles are incapable of going faster than 100. Poorly thought-out regulations are worse than none at all.

If we let nature take its course, we'd find that there are definite physical limits on performance and on ball speed. Just as nobody is going to run the 100-meter dash in five seconds, nobody is going to start hitting routine 400-yard drives (absent extreme conditions of slope or turf hardness and significant increases in clubhead speed). We humans are only able to generate a certain amount of energy, and the transfer of energy is what the collision between club and ball is all about. We can become more efficient through improved body movements and flexibility, but this is an area that is beyond the reach of rules-making bodies.

The first efforts to make rules about equipment — either because something was unsightly or out of fear of unknown properties — labeled such things "not traditional," which is equivalent to calling it revolutionary. The first equipment regulation, written into the code of rules in 1908 by the R&A and adopted by the USGA in 1909, stated in full:

Form and Make of Golf Clubs
The Rules of Golf Committee intimates that it will not sanction any departure from the traditional and accepted form and make of golf club, which in its opinion, consists of a plain shaft and which does not contain any mechanical contrivance, such as a spring.

The clause was broad enough to outlaw virtually anything. This was good enough to stand for many years without challenge, until substantial amounts of money were spent on developing products and more objective guidelines were needed.

The term "traditional" could be used to keep unusual implements and even styles of hitting the ball out of the game, and also to cover for the fear that anything unusual might actually work the way its developers claimed. It remains even today an essential clause in the rules, helping to prevent under the rubric of "Artificial Devices and Unusual Equipment" such brainstorms as laser beams used to aim the club; gyroscopes to keep the club on line; audio feedback devices driven by accelerometers and microgyroscopes that will tell you if your swing is on plane; special glasses to read the greens; sighting devices on the peak of a cap.

The one area of specificity in the regulation was the ban of "any mechanical contrivance, such as a spring." The science of golf was in its infancy — though Professor P.G. Tait had already done groundbreaking work at the University of Edinburgh from 1890 to 1896 — but the rules makers were concerned that a spring in the face might give an extra push to a ball at impact. A silly concern, we know now!!! As for all other aspects of club design, "traditional" seems to cover things well enough.

The phrase "traditional and customary" still appears in the Rules of Golf: "Appendix II (1) (a) ... The club must not be substantially different from the traditional and customary form and make..."

The rules are generally very careful about definitions, giving precise meanings for *stroke, hole, tee, stipulated round, course, caddie, flagstick,* and so on. Not so with *traditional and customary.* In the old days, when rulers went unquestioned, such terms preserved the status quo; if you had any questions about what this meant, you either didn't play golf or must be trying to get away with something you shouldn't. Justice Potter Stewart of the U.S. Supreme Court expressed a similar idea when he wrote of pornography, "I know it when I see it."

Vague as such a clause may be, it does express an important concept. There were times when I leaned on its slender spine in my twenty-six years of monitoring and making rulings as Technical Director of the USGA. Over the years, as rules became more specific and complex, the clause still proved useful. Its broad brush offered in some ways a better approach to thinking about the rules than all the micromanaged specifications we could devise.

I came to realize that the rules should in most cases express principles that cover intents and purposes rather than trying to anticipate every innovation that may arise someday and specify it out of existence. The rules that do this are effective and tend to remain so; the ones that are overly specific often have unintended consequences.

Let's take an example of how the most general rules can operate. A product came up in 1975, the "Polara ball," designed by nongolfers who had some knowledge of aerodynamics (though perhaps not as much as they should have). They created a ball that had dimples only around its equator, being smooth at the poles. I think they believed that dimples created more drag forces than a smooth ball, though in fact dimples are essential to decrease drag forces and generate lift forces that keep the ball airborne longer. They felt that limiting the dimples to where they would be most effective, around the equator of the ball, would provide the best of both worlds, i.e., a ball that would be able to fly but would have less drag resistance so it would fly farther than a ball covered all over with dimples.

The ball flew reasonably well when it was hit with perfect backspin about the (nondimpled) pole axis, though it went about 20 to 25 yards shorter than a standard good ball. But things got freaky when the ball was hit with less than perfect backspin, normally associated with a slice or hook. Then the Polara's design sent the ball into a looping flight, turning right or left depending on the direction of the spin as it was going up, turning back towards the center as the ball descended. The ball corrected a golfer's bad shot in flight; its makers nicknamed it "the Happy Non-Hooker."

Nothing in the rules specifically prevented use of a ball that corrects hooks and slices, but it seems obvious — doesn't it? — that such a ball is a perversion of the intent of the game. Hitting the ball straight requires skill, and we don't want technology to eliminate the need to develop that skill. This is a very different matter than a symmetrically designed ball that may spin less under all conditions — thereby reducing hooks and slices — or a driver that is more forgiving and doesn't twist as much on mishits, thus making the disasters less disastrous. The Polara concept is more in the realm of our Magic Club, the mythical Biggest Big R7-983 Bigfoot that guarantees perfect shots and actually delivers them. Whether or not a specific rule anticipated such a ball, it could not be approved. The people who submitted the product anticipated this reaction and prepared for litigation at the same time as they submitted the ball to the USGA.

This is a perfect example of something that should fall under "traditional and customary" — though that was problematic in this case, because that phrase appears in the clause covering *clubs*, and no one had anticipated that they would have to apply it to a ball. There was, however, a general rule, 37-9 (now 14-3) banning "artificial devices that *might* assist him in making a stroke or in his play" [emphasis mine]. As with "traditional and customary," there are no precise definitions associated with this clause; the preamble to this rule further stated that the USGA "reserves the right, to change the Rules and interpretations regulating clubs and balls at any time." How's that for a trump card? This was exactly the flexibility we needed to do the right thing, to keep the Polara ball from being used in play under the USGA's auspices. (Remember, the USGA can't make you or the PGA Tour do anything; its rules govern its own competitions, and in all other respects depend on the consent of the governed for its authority. It speaks well for its historical performance as a rule maker that so much of the golfing world follows the USGA's and R&A's lead.) The ball was not included on the USGA's list of conforming balls, and a subsequent addition to the Appendix dealing with balls in the rules added a symmetry standard, that the ball "must not be designed, manufactured, or intentionally modified to have properties which differ from those of a spherically symmetrical ball." When it was first put into the rules, this standard had some very well defined specifications that included test procedures; I later removed these, because the rule was so clear in its intent. (When the Pro V1 was introduced, some golfers believed they could get extra distance by aligning the ball along a particular axis on the tee. Whether or not this worked — if it did, the effect was minuscule it was not a violation of the symmetry standard, because the ball was not *designed, manufactured, or intentionally modified* to have such properties. At any rate, the ball was immediately modified to be perfectly symmetrical, though the mistaken belief persisted .)

I'm not so sure the Rules should try to be too specific. When what's nonconforming is tightly defined, the implication is that everything else must be conforming, which is very dangerous and should be avoided, since there is no way to anticipate every potential innovation. The tax laws and their loopholes are examples of regulations where continual upgrading is necessary to sew up the holes found by ingenious people with intent to evade the law's intent.

Something else happens when we write precise specifications that may be meaninglessly restrictive: We give a boost to manufacturers who seize on the regulation as a selling point for what could be inferior products. As soon as the USGA sets a limit, regardless of what it covers or its relevance, manufacturers will engineer their equipment right up to the specified limits, knowing they will have a marketing bonanza. Their pitch to gullible golfers is that something as close to the limit as possible *must* be good, because otherwise the USGA wouldn't have set a limit in the first place.

Some examples of such limitations are the restrictions on head size, shaft length, and the length limitation for a tee. I'm not at all sure why anybody thought it was necessary to restrict tees, but there it is in the rules today: A tee "must not be longer than 4 inches." Four-inch tees are a great benefit to their makers because they break so easily (they're usually inserted about 2 ½ inches into the ground if it's soft enough). Restricting the length of the club (except putters) to 48 inches is another odd decision; if anyone can effectively wield a driving club more than 48 inches long, maintaining control with such a lengthy arc, I'd tip my hat to him instead of outlawing his stick.

"Traditional and customary" works well if it's not abused. For a product to run afoul of it, there must be sound evidence that the innovation or its offspring will have a detrimental effect on the integrity of the game, and therefore should not be permitted even if the rules as written don't cover the specific situation. The Polara ball wasn't nonconforming because it lacked dimples over a specific percentage of its body; it was illegal because its asymmetrical design made it an artificial device that might assist a player in making a stroke or in the play. The rules work best when they effectively describe the intent of the rule.

Shafts, for example, are supposed to be straight. However, very few if any shafts are or can be made perfectly straight, so a specification would have to include the practical problems involved with all the common manufacturing techniques and tolerances for the product and would have to outline precisely the test method with appropriate test tolerances. Such specificity would allow a manufacturer with unique production capabilities to design a shaft that was deliberately crooked but was within the legal limits of tolerance. This manufacturer could then advertise that his shaft has successfully circumvented the USGA's nefarious efforts to keep superior bent-shaft technology out of your hands, and the ruling body couldn't do a thing about it. Better for the rules to state that a shaft must be straight — must be designed with the *intent* of being straight — and leave it at that.

Some companies have taken the limits written into the rules and made a marketing claim around their violation, implying a performance advantage. One such company advertises its nonconforming ball along with some other equipment, hoping to appeal to those who would deliberately purchase an unfair advantage over their competitors. These buyers are not only cheating themselves and their opponents, but are being cheated by the merchant who claims that enhanced performance is the reason for the violation. In fact, the ball is nonconforming because of its size and weight; its actual performance is inferior to that of conforming balls. There's a certain justice in that.

I once had a conversation with a man who was about to send me a grip he had designed for a ruling. I asked him if he'd read the rule covering grips. I was coauthor of this rule, along with Alastair Cochran (my R&A counterpart), and I was very proud of the wording, which I felt was clear and unequivocal, a vast improvement on the precedent-based system we'd been working with prior to the writing of this rule. The rule states in part that the "grip may be tapered but must not have any bulge or waist." The grip designer said that he had read the rule but wanted me to determine after examination if the grip had a bulge and/or a waist. I was concerned by his comment, because I thought there was little room for ambiguity in the rule, so I asked him directly if, in his design, he had included a bulge and waist. My question made him search his conscience, and he replied, "Yes, I did design a bulge into the grip, but I don't think you would have been able to detect it. I will not submit it because I know it doesn't conform." That's where the conversation ended, and he never sent me the grip. He also knew that even if I had not detected the slight bulge and had approved the grip, it would be unwise of him to market the grip as having one. Without that marketing advantage, the product would be a difficult sell.

It is amazing that in most cases, when we are our own judge and use a common-sense interpretation and a touch of conscience, there is little grey area. When we try to circumvent a rule, we are counting on someone else to interpret that rule and thus allow us to evade our responsibility. This is an extension of how in golf we are expected to call penalties on ourselves when we break the rules, while in sports with umpires and referees the athletes try to get away with whatever they can. The presence of the arbiter absolves the player of responsibility to do anything but "just win, baby."

I found therefore that the time spent on explaining the intent of a rule saved hours that would otherwise be spent in trying to enforce some specific measurable limit. Yes, there are times when some specific limits are necessary even though a minor violation is not measurable from a performance point of view. One such limit is the grooves specification. Another is the size and weight specification for balls. Limits were placed on size and weight in 1920 in an effort to control distance; even so, there is only an upper limit on weight and a lower limit on size. (The R&A permitted a smaller ball than the USGA for more than 50 years, a difference that was eliminated in 1990 when the R&A accepted the USGA's 1.68-inch limit.) There have been some attempts since to capture more of the market by introducing a slightly larger ball, but this has not been very successful, and ball size is no longer much of a marketing tool.

Using intent as a way of defining what's permitted is not good for lawyers, because it reduces the need or room for the kind of arguments on which they thrive. But I've found it the best way to approach the rules.

I got called on numerous occasions — five or six, I think — by a gentleman whose putter I had rejected because it had a spirit level (bubble level) encased in its head. This was a clever design, one that incorporated a compartment about the size of a quarter into the top of the putter head. The compartment was circular and almost full of water, with a domed top; there was a black circle inked on the surface of the dome so that when the putter was held perfectly level at address, the bubble would line up with the inked circle. Tilting the club in any direction would result in the bubble wandering away from the marked area.

It was clever, but it ran afoul of several regulations. The level was a device designed to assist in making a stroke, specifically by measuring or gauging conditions that might affect a golfer's play. Also, the rules state that all parts of the club must be fixed, and the fluid in the bubble level was considered a moving part. (This is a good example of a rule that deals with intent. If a piece of the filling for your metal driver comes loose and starts rattling around, the club has a moving part, but it was not intended to be moving and is thus not a violation of the rules. The components of the bubble level were explicitly intended to be a moving part, and thus made it nonconforming.) After many appeals, I advised the gentleman that the putter was not and could not be approved. Still, the calls kept coming, and over time he laid out the history behind the creation of his putter, apparently hoping to win on sympathy what he couldn't win on the merits of the case. He told me:

- The design was conceived in a foxhole in Korea while he was serving our great country.

- Upon returning from the war, he invested all his savings into the development and prototyping of the product.

- His wife had grown distant because of his obsession.

- His wife then left him.

- He was in the hospital with a heart problem as a result of the stress.

- Even in the hospital, all he could think about was the product and nothing else.

How was I supposed to react to all this? I told him that even though it didn't conform to the rules, he could still make it and sell it. He wouldn't be able to use it in a USGA-sanctioned event, but that doesn't mean it might not find a market. I never heard from him again. There's no question I made the proper ruling, but I'm still sad and a little uncomfortable when I think about this man's heartbreak.

Whenever I had to render a decision that something was nonconforming, I would try to speak with the submitter in an effort to break the news to him gently and to make suggestions as to how the design could be modified to make it conform. In many cases these suggestions were accepted, and on numerous occasions when the prototypes were resubmitted the producer told me that the product was actually now better than the original design.

This process of ruling on equipment was one of the most unattractive parts of my job with the USGA. It wasn't because of the difficulty of making decisions — that was relatively easy — but rather the process of going through the same testing over and over, and the endless paperwork that traced every aspect of the submission from first logging-in until final thumbs-up or -down. Fortunately I had good people working with me, which made the task bearable, but I knew I had to be excruciatingly thorough because I did not want to do something wrong or make a decision that I couldn't defend later. Including balls, clubs, gloves, devices such as tees, and everything else, I must have made in excess of 6,000 decisions relating to conformity to the Rules of Golf.

I tried very hard, with some success, to get the USGA and R&A to focus on developing or modifying rules to clearly state their intent, rather than wasting time on rigid technical specifications where marginal violations would be of little consequence. I believed it was better to catch the too-clever who are trying to get away with something than to trap the innocent who fell just outside a tolerance without intending to do so. This seems more in keeping with the spirit of what the game should try to be.

By concentrating on intent, I could better make my way through the philosophy underlying the three basic principles I mentioned earlier, the Traditional, Sameness, and Challenge objectives. The three have evolved over time, but I believe they are the unwritten guidelines that have influenced everyone's thinking about equipment and rules since the start of the 20th century.

The Traditional category covers genuine traditions that are nice to hold onto, but these traditions are hard to define, so this objective mostly arises as a shelter for the fear of the unknown. It is easier to defend a ruling based on tradition because it is so subjective and undefined; as long as you are consistent, you are generally on solid ground. (Still, I did get arguments from people who disagreed with my interpretations of what is traditional, both innovators and members of the USGA's Executive Committee — innovators because they wanted to market a new product, committee members in many cases because they hoped to avoid potential litigation. Some examples were the long putter, holes through the head of a putter, and shafts with spines that require specific orientation to be effective.)

The Traditional clause, when it genuinely relates to "tradition," adds to and is part of the charm of the game — as when it is used to restrict moving parts in clubs, leveling devices, and croquet-style putting but it also overlaps with the desire to make sure that golfers are all playing with the same kind of equipment. So the two objectives, Traditional and Sameness, serve to retain charm and lend order to events where golfers are competing against each other. The "traditional and customary" clause is not used to justify rulings as much as it once was, for a simple reason: Its main purpose is to govern the great unknowns that might radically alter the game in some unspecified way, and with our rapidly expanding base of knowledge and information, there are very few unknowns out there. We can now measure and quantify performance so well that our rules fall more into the Challenge objective; we don't have to call something "untraditional" if we can show that it falls outside our agreed-upon objective standards. We still have the umbrella protection of the rules preamble I quoted above, so there's room for subjectivity if all else fails.

Another part of the preamble puts one of my cherished statements about intent into the rules themselves. After a long fight with those who insisted on specifics, we added wording that states that "where a club is required to have a certain property, it must be designed and manufactured with the intent of having that property." On first reading it looks self-evident, but in fact it captures all those clever innovators who can devise ways to follow literal specifications while designing products that subvert the purpose of the rule.

In 1983, because of my frustration at making rulings based on tradition alone and in trying to be consistent when applying precedent, I proposed we no longer rule on equipment under the Traditional clause but develop a new one which would cover examples of features that were unacceptable. "Traditional and customary" could never be well defined, and thus gave no guidance to potential inventors (though the words are still in the Rules). We introduced a rule to cover and itemize many of the features that had been considered nontraditional in past rulings; "Plain in Shape" best described the grounds for ruling against many of the more outlandish designs we saw and still left plenty of room for both future innovation and opposition to it. The Plain in Shape clause now resides in Appendix II of the Rules of Golf.

With the mission of the Traditional objective changing from a vague shotgun to a more powerful rifle-shot approach, and with the Sameness objective staying statically in place, we are left with the real meat of the equipment rules, the Challenge objective. This is truly where we are able to scientifically and very objectively rule on equipment performance and specifications.

The Overall Distance Standard is a fine example of regulation under the Challenge objective. By setting a limit on how far the ball can travel under test conditions, we no longer have to worry about possible aerodynamic developments, futuristic materials, or magic beans placed inside the ball; if it goes too far, it's nonconforming. The ODS also points up one of the drawbacks of being too specific: ball designers can slide around the regulation by developing balls that conform under the specified test, but go farther when launched under their own optimal conditions. This is why I pressed for an Optimized ODS, and I still believe that would be the only ball regulation the game needs.

The One Ball Rule (technically a "condition" that must be adopted for a competition rather than a formal Rule in effect at all times) is another good adaptation of the Challenge objective. The rule says that "(d)uring a stipulated round, the balls a player plays must be of the same brand and type," which prevents players from using different balls for different conditions within a round. For the average player this would hardly matter, but an elite player could well take advantage of varying performance characteristics. I wrote a memo to the chairman of the committee responsible for equipment regulation in 1975, suggesting that we needed to something about possible ball specialization. I knew that solid two-piece balls flew differently than wound balls, and they might be advantageous on long par-3s into the wind where distance and low spin were especially important. Less than a year after I wrote the memo, a USGA official came striding over to me during a round when I was following a well-known group and said, "Frank, do you know what's going on here? This player is carrying three different balls and using them on different holes depending on the conditions. We have to do something about this." I sent him a copy of the memo I had written several months earlier, and it was decided that we should survey the PGA Tour pros to see if any of them had taken similar advantage, and how they would respond to a rule requiring use of just one kind of ball in a round. Most thought such a rule was necessary, and the Tour adopted the condition soon after. (We learned subsequently that a major manufacturer already had plans to sell a sleeve of balls – I think it was four balls per sleeve – each with different performance properties for specific conditions during a round.)

We don't want the game to become too easy (which is really difficult to do); if golf is to provide the wonderful test of our skills and our character that it should, we have to make certain that equipment doesn't substitute for talent. The Polara ball is a good example of technology that would lessen the challenge of the game. But we must be careful when we use this weapon to limit technology, because not everything that is unfamiliar is bad for the game.

It's important that those who are making the decisions under the Challenge objective understand the real science and engineering behind the process. When people pass judgment on technical matters, they must eliminate their fear that the game is getting away from us (by "us" I mean anyone older than whoever won last week's PGA Tour event). They should also try to learn a little about the subject on which they're ruling. Some of my most frequent and frustrating times came when committee men suggested that we could simply reduce the distance the balls go by eliminating the test tolerance for whatever measure we were using (at the time it was Initial Velocity). The grinding sound you hear as you read this is every engineer in the world gnashing his teeth in unison. This was a suggestion I heard on many, many occasions.

One gentleman once told the guys who were trying to calibrate Iron Byron, the mechanical golfer, before testing balls on that newly acquired machine that they should just put the balls on the tee and "let the f—ers fly." This "LTFF" method became a catchphrase among the technical staff, and it was frequently brought up whenever we were faced with the same kind of thinking.

I am very proud of the work done by the technical staff of the USGA. The technological know-how behind the organization's Research and Test Center is unsurpassed. Thanks to our efforts, the USGA can evaluate equipment performance theoretically and practically in just weeks — a stark contrast to the five years it took for the USGA to decide whether changing to the 1.55-ounce ball permitted in the late 1920s was a good idea or not.

While the technical department can evaluate and explain, it is the Executive Committee that determines how those efforts will be directed.

In the early 1980s, the chairman of the Implements & Ball committee was told by a touring professional that a new ball used on Tour was going up to 25 yards farther than the older model, so there was clearly something wrong with our distance standard. Our test indicated that the new ball was indeed going farther, but by just 1 or 2 yards when using the very precise, well-calibrated mechanical golfer. The pro said we were not testing the ball correctly and that a machine would not produce the same results as professional golfers in the field. He said that people should be testing balls, not machines. We invited the pro to visit Golf House and to help conduct some tests.

The results were amazing; this pro was almost as consistent in reproducing his head speed as the mechanical golfer. We set up the range and installed a special head-speed measuring device. We measured launch angles by eye using a grid-like device and carry distance as well as the roll. The wind and temperature and barometric pressure were recorded. There were four different ball types involved in the test, including the two in question — i.e., the most popular ball on tour and the new version. All the names were inked out, and a technician positioned each ball on the tee before each hit. It took about two hours to conduct the test.

At the conclusion, the data was analyzed and the results given to the professional. The ball that went the farthest by about 5 yards was not used on Tour but was a solid or two-piece ball. The wound ball used on Tour and the new wound ball in question went the same distance on average. In my discussion about the results with the Tour player after the test, I asked him what it was that suggested to him that the new ball was going 25 yards longer. He said, "Well, I thought it was. It just seemed that way."

This is what I faced on a routine basis, and I had to guard against the temptation to react intemperately on many occasions.

Possibly the most contentious ruling I was involved with was the one regarding the thin faces of titanium drivers.

Early in the 20th century, some clever club makers had come up with the idea of building into their clubheads little springs or springy materials behind the face to try to create a trampoline effect when you hit the ball. This was as imaginative as it was ineffective, but they didn't know that then; no turn-of-the-century designer could conceive of measuring time in the tiny fractions needed to describe how little time a ball spends in contact with a club. (See chapter four for the details.) A metal coil could not possibly contract and release in so short a period of time.

Recognizing that these strange little devices might take some of the skill factor out of the game of golf, the governing bodies in 1909 wrote the rule that banned the head of a club from containing any "contrivances such as a spring." The wording indicates that they were worried about these coiled little devils, but were smart enough to anticipate future innovations that might take other forms. No matter what contraption someone came up with — an internal lever? a dynamite charge? if it was an artificial booster of any sort, it would fall under this rule.

In 1984, as metalwoods were becoming popular, I gave some thought to the properties of these clubs and to the potential for mischief in their empty heads. The existing regulation covered artificial aids within the club, but what if some future material acted like a spring all by itself? Would that still be considered a contrivance? I didn't know for sure what metallurgists and engineers might come up with, but it seemed prudent to clarify the current rule to cover it. I recommended we introduce a rule to cover "springlike effect." Now it wouldn't matter what caused the effect, whether it was a mechanical device or something intrinsic to the material used in the club; if it had the *effect* of a spring, it was against the rules.

When I got the call from a leading manufacturer that I described in chapter three, the one alerting me to a possible springlike effect in some large titanium drivers, we devised a cannon test to determine whether the faces were actually deforming and recovering during the .00045 seconds that the ball is in contact with the club.

We found that in fact the titanium heads with thin faces did enhance ball velocity over all other heads, be they wooden, steel, or even first-generation titanium. In all other cases the coefficient of restitution (COR) was dependent almost totally on the resilience of the ball, and in no case did the head or face contribute to this ball speed other than lending its weight, velocity, and hardness to the collision. In other words, these clubs did not have any springlike effect.

To develop a standard test, rather than test clubs we decided to demonstrate the phenomenon in a neutral context. We built an air cannon and machined cavities into the back of circular plates of titanium. At the base of the cavity was a very thin face, which represented a clubface surrounded by a weighted ring of titanium. The total weight of this platelike structure was equivalent to that of a standard driver head (7 ounces). We then fired a ball at the plate, sitting on a pedestal, hitting it right in the center of the thin face, and compared the ball return speed to plates of the same weight but without the cavity.

The result indicated that the thin face did indeed enhance the ball velocity as expected.

Immediately after our tests, I reported to the directors of the USGA that the faces of these new clubs were demonstrating a distinct springlike effect in violation of the rules. It wasn't a deliberate violation; the manufacturers were trying to make all the walls thinner to increase the perimeter weighting, trying to maximize the size of the sweet spot and the forgiveness factor. They did not even know that they were creating this little boost to the ball's velocity; it was a byproduct, but it was a violation nonetheless. I remember talking to a gentleman at Callaway and advising him that his Great Big Berthas had springlike effect in the face. He denied it — but said that some Japanese manufacturers had it in their clubs and we (the USGA) should do something about it.

Unfortunately, I could not persuade our committee to stand firm and enforce the rules. The rules clearly state that a club may not have "the effect of a spring." An ultrathin titanium face has exactly that effect. I warned the committee that there would be a quantum jump in the distance that pros drive the ball if we did not enforce the rule. I suggested we provide a grace period of six years or more for those clubs already on the market — though where distance was of greatest concern, on the PGA Tour, the rule could be enforced immediately and within weeks. There was good reason for a generous grace period, but production had to be stopped. It was obvious from test data that the springlike effect was going to increase the pros' distance significantly. The actual potential increase was unknown, but I knew the Overall Distance Standard would be compromised in its intent if the club could now help project the ball faster.

It was evident that the organization wanted to avoid another lawsuit like the Ping suit over grooves, so they proposed a COR limit that would be carefully tailored to leave all existing clubs as conforming. The rule stating "no effect of a spring" would not change. But a COR that included some springlike effect would be permitted. (No smoking, but six cigarettes are OK.)

I was asked in a meeting if the distance increase would be minimal if the proposed COR limit of 0.83 was adopted. I said, emphatically, that it would not be minimal. In fact, I suggested a possible increase of 18 to 25 yards. I was not sure what the total effect might be, but I did know that we had entered a new era where, for the first time, the face of a club would actually enhance the speed of a ball at impact. As it turned out, the titanium head in conjunction with the newly formulated solid core balls allowed drives to be launched closer than ever to optimum conditions. This next generation of Tour balls were like super Pinnacles or TopFlites with three not two layers, the outermost being very thin and soft to allow for control around the green. One USGA man had predicted to me that manufacturers would one day develop a Pinnacle or TopFlite that was acceptable to the pros despite its solid construction. This happened first with Bridgestone's Precept three-piece ball, followed by Titleist with its Pro V1. In conjunction with the springlike effect, this has allowed pro golfers to increase their total driving distance by about 25 yards on average. The average annual increase on Tour jumped from 1 foot per year, which had been the rate for almost thirty years of data collection prior to 1996, to nearly 8 feet per year over the following nine years as golfers changed their equipment to optimize performance.

I couldn't have predicted that increase exactly, but I knew there would be a significant difference in performance. I was a little upset at being asked to compromise the enforcement of a rule I had written, and especially at being told that I was not really interpreting it correctly. Perhaps I should have just accepted it and kept my mouth shut. This is not my nature.

Some people don't like to hear the truth or anything that is not in line with their chosen strategies. The problem is that the decision was wrenching. The USGA had been openly trying to control distance increases, while at the same time avoiding litigation. Here those objectives were in conflict, and unfortunately, the "potential for litigation" side of the scale won. This was by all observations a blatant case where potential legal consequences affected decisions more than the best interests of the game. Worse, the USGA has been playing catch-up ever since this disaster, introducing or proposing rules to make up for this error, most of which hurt the average golfer more than the initial restriction would have.

Regardless, the USGA decided that it was better to set a COR limit at the existing state of the art than to risk a lawsuit. They okayed a certain amount of springlike effect, setting off an arms race among manufacturers and the pros who used their products — because, after all, who wants to compete with substandard artillery? Considering all the hot air that has been expended on the problem of distance in the ten years since this particular barn door was left unlocked, maybe a little more legal gumption would have been better.

Here, too, a clear rule based on intent would have been more effective than the scientifically derived specification has proved to be. "No effect of a spring" is clear; since the initial clubs that had this effect came about it unintentionally, they would get a grace period before being removed from the market, though production would have to stop. (Once you've been informed that you're building a club with springlike effect, continuing to manufacture it means you are doing so with intent.) Setting a COR limit of 0.83 has been more problematic, since you must allow for a test tolerance, and some manufacturers will incorporate that tolerance in their designs (inevitably resulting in nonconforming specimens within their manufacturing lots).

Intent really does point the way to the best regulations we can create.

There is something good about maintaining some level of constancy in life. Protecting traditions enables our grandfathers to recognize the game our grandchildren will play. Golf is a game that celebrates its past along with its present; we want to walk the fairways where Hogan, Jones, Vardon, and Morris strode, enjoy the presence of Jack Nicklaus, Gary Player, and Arnold Palmer for what they have done as we still try to do, and to see Woods, Sorenstam, Mickelson, and Els battle the standards set by their predecessors.

But preserving tradition poses difficulties as well. One man's tradition is another man's impediment. It was once traditional to tee one's ball upon a small mound of damp sand. It was once traditional to have no distance markings of any kind on a golf course, requiring players to gauge their shots with their eyeballs or those of their caddies only. Wooden pegs and EMDs (Electronic Measuring Devices) are accepted now, but could have been banned if tradition governed the game alone. The game is not static, as static implies inactive. The game is active and dynamic; it needs to keep pace with the times and lifestyles, and any attempt to preserve it by putting it in a bottle would be equivalent to cutting off the oxygen to a living creature. It is the challenge we need to preserve and protect. To protect it first requires an understanding of what it is and how it makes us crave it. Only with this understanding will we be able to protect it without causing damage to the game and to ourselves.

Rules are essential to any organized activity, lending order and preserving integrity. We voluntarily abide by those rules because they make intuitive sense to us. It's when the rules makers stray from the essence of what they're trying to protect, and for whom, that things go wrong.

Let's play by the rules and lobby to change those that don't make intuitive sense. The game will be better for it.

Golf does not need to be as rigid as NASCAR, where performance is based on mechanical design and extremely precise specifications are needed. There is room — indeed, there is a need — for the flexibility provided by the phrase "traditional and customary." The rules do embrace complexity; some of the standards encoded within them are based on science as sophisticated as any in the world of sport. But just in case something comes along that can't be anticipated, "Traditional and Customary" is still there to save the game of golf from potential harm.

That's good enough for me.

CHAPTER SEVEN: Saving the Game

Golf is one of the oldest and most wonderful sports activities man has access to, and it has served us well. We have derived pleasure and humility, excitement and therapy, warmth and anger, but most importantly the opportunity for self-evaluation that lies subconsciously within our urge to play the game. Despite these good things, all is not rosy in the land of golf.

According to the National Golf Foundation, in 1997 there were thirteen-and-a-half million adult core golfers (those who play eight or more rounds a year) in the United States. In 2005, the most recent year for which we have data, there were one million fewer. The total number of golfers who play at least one round a year is hovering around 25 million, depending on who is counting, but they're not developing the steady habit that would bring them into the core group. The number of rounds played in the U.S. has been declining steadily from a high of approximately 550 million per year in 1997 to about 480 million in 2006.

Why should we care? If the trend continues, we may find in a few years that it's easier to get a tee time, and our rounds might be quicker when we do go out to the course. We won't have to wait as other people line up their putts like they've seen on television or think long and hard about club selection when they hit most of their clubs the same (badly) or search for their wayward shots without having the courtesy to wave us through.

As we continue to discourage others from playing our game, we'll keep them from discovering the satisfaction we feel when we hit good shots or record good scores or even just spend the time outdoors with good companions, and so we'll help prevent the masses from becoming addicts like ourselves.

Still, most of us learn as civilized people that there's something nice about sharing and selfish about keeping good stuff to ourselves. If a harmless addiction can be a good thing and a source of therapy and pleasure, then golf is certainly one place to find it.

If we let participation continue to decline without trying to nurture our game and bring new people in, then the things we have today that are good may not be as good in the future. Course conditions may decline for lack of qualified greenkeepers and lowered maintenance budgets. This isn't necessarily a bad thing, since too many courses are groomed in a misguided effort to mimic Augusta National, but it will definitely change the experience for us in ways we don't expect. With fewer people playing, courses will close down and be sold for housing or commercial development, especially those extremely valuable pieces of real estate surrounding our suburban homes; the remaining courses will face the same crowding problems we face now. Because they're viewed as playgrounds for the rich though five minutes at a muni will put the lie to this stereotype golf courses will come under increasing pressure from political forces, through zoning restrictions or crackdowns on the use of water and pesticides, all because we've isolated ourselves by treating the game as a club that's not accepting new members.

The game as a whole has been rudderless, its path set by a disparate group of individual agendas designed for economic gain. Making money and respecting the game can go hand in hand; there are some who truly love the game while benefiting financially from it. In most cases, however, the exploitation is not in the game's long-term interest, and we will suffer for the failure to think and look beyond the next profit/loss statement.

The professional Tours provide entertainment for paying customers and television viewers, but they put undue focus on a tiny elite fraction of the golf universe. Players in the top 1 percent, buoyed by improved workout regimens and better understanding of launch conditions, can hit the ball farther than ever before. Such gains are promoted by the Tours and by equipment manufacturers hoping the average golfer will ignore the professionals' hours of exercise and practice and simply try to buy those same results.

As tournament courses grow longer and harder, developers and architects feel obliged to build "championship courses" just so they can trumpet that phrase in their housing prospectuses. The costs to build and maintain such elephantine layouts have grown beyond reason. Those expenses are especially difficult to justify once the developer has met his home lot sales goals, whereupon he kindly donates the high-maintenance course to those lucky homeowners, a surprising percentage of whom don't play golf.

Even if this latter group did play golf, they would find themselves disheartened by the challenge their home course presents. Water features make for beautiful photographs in the brochure and pleasant backyard views, but a reliance on lakes and culverts in the line of play create a repetitive version of the game that grows expensive as the price of lost balls rises. ("The difference between a sand trap and water," said Bobby Jones, "is like the difference between a car crash and a plane crash.") Forward sets of tees are little help if the green site is designed to test the skills of a pro, with copious hazards and voluptuous contours that require pinpoint accuracy on approach. It's not enough to build a tough course and then retrofit the average player into it; the appropriate level of difficulty must be considered in every decision an architect makes, from the placement of hazards to the grading of the land.

Compounding the problem, the more hazards and contours there are, the more expensive the course will be to maintain. The planners don't always take this into account, and so those added costs get passed on to those who use the course. The price of a round (or a membership) becomes a detriment when someone is deciding if he wants to keep playing the game – or to take it up in the first place. Those courses also take longer to play, especially when the high price leads the irrational golfer to play from the wrong tees in order to "see the whole course" and get full value for the hefty investment. This foolish decision leads to more shots and more difficult shots, further eroding the enjoyment level for all.

Architects say they can only build the courses that developers want. Developers say they are giving the public what will sell. Golfers know vaguely that they're dissatisfied, but can't exactly say why. And nobody is looking at the problem from an overall perspective.

If golf is a drug and playing it an addiction, we are doing a lousy job as pushers. We are not getting new users hooked, and we're supplying an inferior product to our existing market.

If the individual profit motive isn't enough to ensure the extended health of the game, who should be watching out for it?

Apparently not the USGA; its charter states that its objective is to administer the rules, run championships, and otherwise do what is in the best interests of the game. While the last part could be interpreted broadly, there is nothing explicit that says it should promote the growth of the game. Nonetheless, I would argue, its success as the game's guardian can be measured by how well it exposes the game to all, and whether it increases the numbers of those who make it a part of their lives. The organization has launched membership campaigns whose benefits to its members are extremely unclear. (They used to receive an excellent magazine, *Golf Journal*, but it was discontinued in 2003.) It has entered into sponsorships with American Express, Lexus, and Rolex, forfeiting the amateur status that was an essential part of its position overseeing the integrity of the game. Unless it has substantial costs of which we are not aware, the USGA's coffers should be full to bursting, and we will be most interested to see what it does with the money. Helping the game grow — the game, not its membership rolls —would be a worthwhile investment of those dollars.

Maybe the PGA of America — the association of teaching professionals — is an appropriate organization to help push our drug into new corners, to assure an ongoing market for its lessons and products. Maybe it should be the club owners and their association, or the developers, or the manufacturers, or the magazines, or teachers, or architects, or even the PGA Tour. These groups would all benefit from increased participation, so perhaps everybody involved in golf should feel some responsibility to take pro bono actions that will aid the long-term health of the game and ensure that the professions they enjoy will exist and prosper for the indefinite future. Devoting a portion of our efforts to the betterment of the future is one way to pay back those whose work in the past made our lives possible.

The game today has some serious problems, and if we don't start making changes it will continue to decline. There will be fewer viewers, decreased sponsorship, lower beer sales on the course or at the nineteenth hole, fewer teaching opportunities, no need for as many golf balls or clubs, increased club owner association dues to make up for the decrease in clubs, less need for architects as course closings surpass openings, and other enticements will take the place of golf courses for developers to lure buyers to their gated webs.

We cannot keep picking the fruit without fertilizing the tree now and again. It is time to tend the tree, to feed the goose whose golden eggs we roll across the manicured green.

Arthur D. Little and his wife, Jann Leeming, commissioned a study in 2005 to help identify how golfers — other than the fractional elite segment — actually play the game, what attracts them to it, and what detracts from their experience of it. My firm, Frankly Consulting, undertook the study, putting a full-length questionnaire on a linked website. In a matter of six weeks we had 18,400 responses from concerned golfers in forty-four countries, 14,400 responses from the U.S. alone. Among the topics covered were whether the challenge presented to the average golfer was appropriate and, if not, how to modify existing courses or design new ones that would better address his needs and desires.

The conclusions from the study are not surprising to most people concerned about the game's health. We intuitively know that there are problems with cost, slow play, lack of beginner facilities (no equivalent of skiing's "bunny slopes"), and length (which affects both cost and speed of play). The study's report quantifies these concerns. Some of the highlighted issues we need to address are:

- Most golf courses are designed for the scratch golfer, but only 0.65 percent of the golfing population plays to scratch or better.

- Most golfers attempt to play a course that is too long; the average golfer's preference is to play a course of 6,200 yards for men, under 5,000 for women.

- The two greatest deterrents to developing an addiction to golf are cost and time.

- Beginners need a place to play where they can experience the game without being frightened away, either through difficulty of the course or by the regular golfers breathing down their necks.

We all have a responsibility for the health of golf, even those of us who do nothing more than pay a green fee and play the game. I hope we will all take the following eight steps to heart, as building blocks for the future of the game we love.

1. UNDERSTAND THE TRUE GAME.

Golf is a game played between opponents and friends, between our efforts and the conditions, between our plans and the course, but mostly between our desires and our capabilities. It is one of the finest methods of self-evaluation ever created, one that takes our measure every time we step up to the first tee.

If we know this and believe it, then we can relax about a lot of things that seem so important now. We don't need the absolute latest and finest piece of technology in our hands, because we're evaluating ourselves, not our equipment maker. It won't bother us if the playing surface isn't tended to a billiard-table sheen, because our mission is to deal with whatever we may find on the greensward. Palatial clubhouses with catering facilities for two hundred mean nothing to our struggle to shave a stroke or two from our lifetime best.

The game is not the trappings. Don't get caught up in all the externals. Golf is every bit as alive on a sheep-tended pasture course as it is at the U.S. Open.

2. Know that the Magic Is in You.

We've all done it: Our playing partner hits a booming drive, and our first reaction is not, "Nice swing!" but rather, "Lemme see that club! Where'd you get it?"

It's a little insulting, really. The club did nothing special, and it could as easily have topped the ball into the gunk if that had been the path we gave it. But we ooh and aah over the new equipment, and we enshrine under glass the clubs that hit famous shots as though they were relics of the saints.

We want to believe in magic. We want to take full credit for our best results, but we want a little extracurricular boost from our implements, assistance that's our due for all the bad breaks we endure so stoically.

Marketers and manufacturers play to our belief in magic. They know that we want to be better golfers than we are, and they offer us shortcuts to greater distance, purer shots, and lower scores. Never mind that those promised gains ultimately prove as elusive as the winning selection in the Big Game lottery; for a while we believe, and for a while we see results even if they're not there.

Slowly, golfers are coming to recognize that we're being sold more hope than substance. Every year brings the introduction of new clubs, new breakthroughs in technology, new buzzwords to drop in conversation and show off to your friends. But the laws of physics don't change from year to year, and breakthroughs don't arrive on a marketer's timetable. If last year's clubs were so wonderful and advanced and amazing, how can this year's be so much better still?

The placebo effect is real; a medicine we believe in will help us feel better, even if it's just a sugar pill. And a new driver we have confidence in will help us swing more smoothly, and this may even give us that eternally-sought 20 extra yards (on occasion).

But the magic isn't in the club, which will get to know the thirteen nonmagic clubs in your bag and will soon start swinging just like those traitorous others. The magic is in the *belief.* It's in us. When we realize this, we'll stop throwing large sums of money after illusory improvements, and we'll relax in the knowledge that our clubs and balls are good and well-made and that we don't need to chase mirages. The charm of looking for the magic wand is compelling, but if we ever did find it we would only be disappointed, as it would take away our reason for playing the game in the first place.

3. PLAY THE RIGHT SET OF TEES.

Ego is a powerful impediment to an enjoyable golf game.

Here's a fact: One of the most frequently cited reasons for giving up the game, according to our survey, was that it takes too long.

Here's another fact: The average male golfer who shoots between 90 and 95 drives the ball 192 yards — but thinks he drives it 230–240. (Women are not immune to this: their numbers are 145 and 175 respectively.)

Yet how often does this average golfer play from too far back, because he "wants to see the whole course"? Or because he's fallen into a foursome with one long hitter, and so he figures he'll play "where the big boys play"? Conversely, how rare is it for this golfer, who has seen his scores constantly rise because of the pressure the course is putting on his game (more on this later), to move *up* to the gold tees?

Playing from the wrong tees is a sure way to make the day longer (because of the time needed for recovery shots, assuming the ball can be found at all), more expensive (from the more difficult carries over water), and more frustrating for all, especially the foursome behind you.

If your average drive is 192, and your average 6-iron is 150, then a 342-yard par-four is a good challenge for you — even if your low-handicap partners are playing the same hole at 430 yards (265 and 165). A good rule of thumb is that *par should be an achievable goal for you on every hole.* If you can't reach the green on an average par-four with your maximum drive and your maximum second shot, you're playing from the wrong tee.

Move up, and discover the joy of hitting a mid-iron into a green again, getting close enough to putt for birdie. When every shot no longer requires your *absolute* best swing, you'll have more confidence and be more likely to make that great swing in the first place.

Course owners can help out here. Offer players an incentive to move up: Buy a round of drinks at the nineteenth hole for any foursome that plays from one tee forward of its usual set and finishes the round in four hours or less. They'll probably enjoy it so much that they'll move up on their own next time, and you'll find more golfers finishing more rounds at a reasonable pace, and they'll come back more often.

At the Old Course in St. Andrews, tee markers are set out for each day's play, and visiting golfers need special permission to play from the back (medal) tees. You'll probably wind up playing the course at about 6,300 yards. Have you ever heard anyone who played there complain that the course was too easy for them? This, too, is a possible model for course operators, putting out one set of tee markers for the day and asking all golfers to play from them. (The near-scratch player can obtain permission to play from the longer medal markers by showing he can play from them in under four hours.)

We're all on the course together, and you can help keep things moving by choosing the appropriate challenge for your real game. As the scorecard at one of the R&A medals I've played in reminds us, "Your position on the course is immediately behind the group in front of you, NOT immediately in front of the group behind you."

4. BUILD FASTER COURSES.

In Scotland, traditionally, a round of golf was expected to take three hours and fifteen minutes, no longer. Americans are always shocked to hear this, as we've grown accustomed to thinking of four hours as an unattainable goal at so many of our courses. It helps greatly that those Scottish rounds are usually match play, not medal, so no one's obsessed with holing out and recording every stroke once a hole is lost; also, they're playing on courses where the walking is easy because they're relatively flat and the next tee is just a few steps from the edge of the green. Further, links courses don't have a lot of trees, which make tracking and finding a bad shot more difficult, especially in autumn.

Slow play is not always the fault of the golfer. (Though, to be sure, we could all benefit from the following: (1) Play ready golf; (2) Get your distances on the way to your ball, don't go to it and then start looking around; (3) Line up your putts while you're waiting for your turn; (4) One practice swing is plenty, if not too many; (5) Pros have extensive preshot routines; most of us are just stalling.) The way we build golf courses today contributes to the length of a round, and architects and developers should consider this at the start of a project.

Too many courses require the use of golf carts, because the trek from green to tee can seemingly take us from one zip code to another. (The cart has become so much a part of American golf, and so many courses couldn't be played without them, that it's only a matter of time before golfers' legs atrophy from lack of use and become as vestigial as the appendix.) Hazards should be appropriate to the golfers who'll be playing the course; an island green may be fun for the pros, but it's not something the average handicap player wants to see on a regular basis. (Courses should be built for those who play them, not for those who'll talk about them while they're selling property.) The phrase "championship course" should be banished from the game, unless it's describing a place where an actual championship has been or will be held.

Short grass should be encouraged and long grass resisted, unless the pro Tour is visiting. Penal rough leads to delays for finding balls, and uninspiring shot choices for getting out of it. (One of Alister Mackenzie's dictates for the ideal golf course is that "There should be a complete absence of the annoyance and irritation caused by the necessity of searching for lost balls.") Around the greens, short grass makes little pitches tougher for the average player, and adds an element of doubt as to what type of shot to play (pitch, chip, putt, bump-and-run). Such choices make the game more interesting, more fun – certainly more fun than a long series of throw-the-dart approach shots that must clear bunkers and land and stick on the green.

Courses should be built with the average golfer in mind, and then adapted (if need be) to increase the challenge for the scratch or professional player, not the other way around.

5. Think Outside the Eighteen.

With the number of rounds declining, we need to find ways to lure back the golfer who can't or won't devote the hours needed to play eighteen holes. One way to do this would be to route a course in three loops of six holes rather than two of nine. The player could then choose from three possible lengths — six holes, twelve, or eighteen — which would be priced accordingly. One size does not fit all; it's easier for a wavering golfer to find the time to play if that time comes in small, medium, and large.

6. Give Back to the Game.

Perhaps the greatest problem facing golf is that it's such a hard game to learn at first, especially on the courses that are being built today. The beginning golfer who struggles to get the ball airborne has no chance of hitting a green that's pushed up and ringed with sand, regardless of where the tees are.

But the true addiction to golf can only be acquired on the course; the range just isn't good enough. The aspiring golfer needs to see the ball travel in the right direction, watch it land where it's supposed to go, and hear it rattle home into the cup if he is to develop that itch to do it again and better.

Course operators would be wise to build "bunny slopes" — loops of a few holes that can be played by novice golfers as a prelude to advancing to the full course itself. If you have a professional on staff and a practice facility, reach out to the community and offer lessons at inexpensive group rates, then turn these neo-golfers loose on their own abbreviated layout for as long as they wish. (The loop could be priced by time, so that one fee would allow someone to go around and around for a set number of hours.) If land is an issue, close the driving range for part of the day and use the target greens to create a beginners' course. Give student discounts and publicize this at local schools. Make a big deal of those golfers who graduate to the big course; these are your future regular customers, and they and their children are the future of the game.

7. Remember that the Customer Has the Power.

In the last three decades, we've seen some remarkable boom and bust cycles in golf. We've seen equipment change and courses change and maintenance standards change; we haven't seen handicaps change much, but that's another story.

We've certainly seen prices change. Callaway's Big Bertha ushered in the era of the high-tech, high-dollar driver, and its success drew many competitors into the market. Daily-fee courses were built to provide the "country club for a day" experience, with green fees that ticked steadily upward into the annual-dues range. These business models require a constant infusion of consumers willing to spend a lot for what they consider the best.

Marketers dream of finding a product for which demand increases as prices rise. For a while, golf fit that model, but the last decade has seen a shakeout in the industry. At a recent Golf 2020 Summit — a convocation intended to discuss ways to double participation by the year 2020 — the final report revolved around identifying and locating the "best customer," that person who will prop up the troubled businesses by spending, spending, spending. The assumption was that the product is good enough, we just need to find better consumers.

If the product were good enough, people would find the time for it. The quest to squeeze one more drop of blood from the "best customer" is futile, as he is already bleeding profusely.

We, the golfers, don't owe anybody our business. If an equipment company keeps changing its models and presents each minimal (or nonexistent) improvement as a new paradigm, we don't have to buy it. If a course treats us as though we're doing it a favor by showing up and playing there, we can go elsewhere. If a design frustrates us with an endless succession of near-impossible challenges, we can choose not to go back.

Similarly, if the experience we have at a golf course is wonderful, if we walk away wishing we could go right back out and start over, if the challenge is appropriate and sufficient and the pace is pleasing, we can go back and tell our friends and keep it a thriving enterprise. (And if its response is to jack up its prices two- and three-fold, we can look for someplace new.) A happy golfer is the best advertising you can have.

The consumer has the power to make a business succeed. We make choices every time we set out to play. Reward the good stuff and stay away from the exploiters.

8. GET BACK TO BASICS.

Before we all thought about golf as a business, we recognized it as a wonderful game. We laid out courses so that we could enjoy it, and we formed clubs and associations so that we could get together regularly with our friends and share it.

Once we turned golf into a commodity, we let all sorts of problems into the game. We decided that bigger is always better. We considered it something to use for another purpose — making money, showing off our wealth, impressing clients — and we opened it up to those who don't care about it at all but who want something from us and are manipulating our desires so they can get it from us.

Not everything and everyone who makes money from golf is bad, but when the money-making is the sole purpose, the results leave the game in a weaker place — which is where we find ourselves today.

Fortunately, there are good things happening too. Starting in 1999, we've seen the wildly successful launch of the Bandon Dunes golf resort on the Oregon coast. We've seen a trend among architects to build courses that avoid moving large quantities of earth, instead letting the land guide the creative hand. We've seen courses embrace the example of the great linksland sites in Scotland and Ireland, with open space and greens that can be approached by running a shot along the ground as well as through the air. These things are all wonderful for the game, as they make it accessible for players of many levels of skill.

The Bandon example is an especially interesting one. According to the book *Dream Golf,* by Stephen Goodwin, Bandon's developer, Mike Keiser, didn't go looking for a large population area into which he could shoehorn a golf course. He looked for the best land he could find for golf and set out to build the kind of playable, enjoyable course that he would want to revisit again and again. He didn't do it because his business advisors told him it would be a good strategy; he did it because it was the right way to express the values of the game. He wasn't building homesites; he wasn't selling real estate. He was building golf courses. Again and again he put commercial considerations aside — especially when he declared that there would be no golf carts except for people with disabilities — and looked for ways to focus and enhance the golf experience. Today Bandon has three courses, with a fourth in the works, and it has become a must-play destination without ever hosting a big professional tournament. Golfers who travel there quickly see that it's all about the golf. And that turned out to be the best commercial approach of all. I haven't had the chance to see it for myself, but I look forward to getting out there one day soon to see if it's everything I've heard.

The game of golf is a big and beautiful thing. It instills self-reliance, rewards excellence that is sought through honest effort, can be enjoyed by young and old, men and women, rich and poor, and is at heart as simple as whacking a little round object with a stick. It is as possessing, obsessing, bewitching, and beguiling a pastime as man has ever devised. It's ours to enjoy, and ours to pass along in as good a shape as we found it, and maybe better. We proclaim the game our own every time we put a tee in the ground, every time we draw a club back in hope and anticipation.

We can all make a difference. The ball is waiting.

Just hit it!

ABOUT THE AUTHORS

FRANK THOMAS has spent much of his life as one of the guardians of the game of golf, and today he is making it his mission to help golfers around the world.

In his twenty-six years as Technical Director of the United States Golf Association, he was responsible for testing and ruling on the acceptability of every new club and ball. Since leaving the USGA in 2000, he has devoted his efforts and passion to educating consumers about golf technology and empowering them to make better decisions about equipment. His opinions on the game have appeared on the Op-Ed page of *The New York Times*, and he is Technical Advisor to *Golf Digest* as well as Chief Technical Advisor to The Golf Channel. His honest and straightforward evaluations of today's technology reach millions of consumers through The Golf Channel and his website www.franklygolf.com.

JEFF NEUMAN is a writer, editor, and consultant on many subjects including golf. His articles have appeared in *The New York Times, Links Magazine, Private Clubs,* and a variety of other publications. He is co-author (with Lorne Rubenstein) of *A Disorderly Compendium of Golf.* He lives in New York City.